THE GREAT AMERICAN
READING MACHINE

THE GREAT AMERICAN READING MACHINE

DAVID J. YARINGTON

HAYDEN BOOK COMPANY, INC.
Rochelle Park, New Jersey

To my parents,
Dr. and Mrs. Charles Yarington

LB
1050
Y37

Library of Congress Cataloging in Publication Data

Yarington, David Jon.
The great American reading machine.

Includes index.
1. Reading—United States.   I. Title.
LB1050.Y37   428'.4'0973   77-18186
ISBN   0-8104-5999-X
ISBN   0-8104-5998-1   pbk.

Printed in the United States of America

1	2	3	4	5	6	7	8	9	PRINTING

78 79 80 81 82 83 84 85 86   YEAR

PREFACE

The focus of this book is on what most people consider the most important school responsibility — the teaching of reading. It's a book for parents and teachers, who know that the job is not being done well, but who don't know why not and who are puzzled about why the "all-out national commitment to reading improvement" has for a decade brought lots of promises but few successes.

Why is it that we never hear at what "level" Johnny is mathing or sciencing or social studying, but if someone is reading "below grade level," watch out! Why do so many kids continue to read about Dick and Jane and Spot and ... ? Why does "remedial reading" infest the curriculum right up into college? Why is it that in every part of the country minority children do poorly in reading test scores? Why is it so hard to find out how your child is reading? ("Well, he's in book 2.1" and "She's reading right on level" seem to be the only kinds of responses we get. How parents translate that kind of information into how well their children read is a mystery.)

This book is about how reading is taught and not taught. It insists that the reading problem is the direct outgrowth of what I've identified as The Great American Reading Machine — the interlocking mutual self-interest created over the years among government agencies (local, state, and federal), textbook publishers (particularly of basal readers), reading experts (professors in schools of education, reading specialists in the schools, and private operators of reading programs), language arts coordinators, and classroom teachers. They all have such high personal and financial stakes in the reading business — in selling and defending their expertise — that they don't recognize (and wouldn't admit) that *they* are the primary cause of the nation's reading crisis. The book is a detailed analysis of just why The Machine is the culprit, and it suggests a program of action that could bring significant changes.

As a professional who has been involved in the training of reading teachers for almost 15 years, I make no claim to objectivity. My biases will be evident in the pages that follow. It is not my purpose to convince the reader that any one method of teaching reading is better than any other. My purpose is to make clear that the real problem is The Great American Reading Machine. It inhibits good teaching, perpetuates the use of poor materials, and creates a climate that encourages rigid adherence to one approach or another — or abrupt switches from one to another — without any sound bases for either behavior. Understanding the reasons for this state of affairs is the first step in beginning to find solutions. I do not provide all the answers, but I feel I am asking the right questions.

DAVID J. YARINGTON

ACKNOWLEDGMENTS

The writing of this book has taken many years. Many people have been involved in one way or another. I am grateful to Dwight Allen, Marge Andrews, Barnes Boffey, Bob Boynton, Dian Buck, Marcia Clapp, Sister Diane Dehn, Elaine Duemler, Jim Duggins, Dick Earle, Martha Evans, Sister Irene Therese Henze, Donna Johnson, Burton Lasky, Walter Pauk, Dick Schaye, Bill Schreck, and Marti Yarington for all their help. I thank also all the students and professors who have influenced me over the years.

D.J.Y.

CONTENTS

THE GREAT AMERICAN READING MACHINE

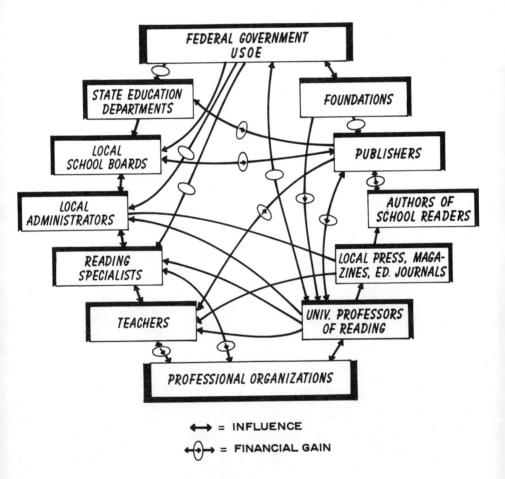

ONE

READING, IN PERSPECTIVE

Ask anyone how well he or she reads and the answer is often "not as well or as fast as I should." Many of us think we have reading problems of one sort or another. Partly because so many children are passing through the public school system without really learning to read, teaching children to read is universally considered the most important task of American elementary schools. Huge quantities of statistics about how well this task is being carried out are constantly issued by local and state school systems, by independent testing agencies, and by the U.S. Office of Education, among other sources. Consider the national statistics.

In 1969, James E. Allen Jr., the late U.S. Commissioner of Education, reported the following U.S. Office of Education statistics:

1. One out of every four students nationwide has significant reading deficiencies.
2. In large city school systems up to one-half the students read below expectations.
3. There are more than three million illiterates in our adult population.
4. About one-half of the unemployed youth in New York City, ages 16–21, are functionally illiterate.
5. Three-quarters of the juvenile offenders in New York City are 2 or more years behind in reading.
6. In a recent U.S. Armed Forces program called "Project 100,000," 68.2 percent of the young men fell below grade 7 in reading and academic ability.

At that time, Allen called for national commitment to a "Right to Read" program designed to solve the illiteracy problem in 10 years.[1] A National Reading Council was formed and approved by President Nixon, who made his wife honorary chairperson. The council consisted of well-known citizens who had the tasks of rallying the country around the cause of reading and of raising money. Since no federal funds were appropriated for the council, it quietly died, but not before it funded an important survey.

Louis Harris and Associates was contracted by the council in 1970 to conduct a poll of illiteracy in the United States. Interviewers asked a total of 1,482 individuals across the country to fill out five application forms—an innovative and practical test of reading skills. One of Harris's conclusions, based on the same sort of sampling technique used to rate television shows and count the number of people who watch them, was that *over 18 million people could not correctly complete an application for Medicaid.*[2]

According to the Bureau of Census, in 1970 there were almost two million persons 25 years old and over who had not completed a single year of school. In the same age group there were over 14 million persons who had not completed more than 8 years of school.[3] For years, illiteracy was judged by census statistics. These data assume that an individual who has completed a given number of years of school has learned to read. We know that poor readers are passed on from grade to grade and eventually graduate in many school systems. So census statistics are at best underestimates of the number of illiterates.

The most extensive, well-designed, large-scale study of functional literacy ever conducted is the National Assessment of Educational Progress (NAEP), a project of the Education Commission of the States, based in Denver, Colorado. The NAEP has been funded by the U.S. Office of Education at a multimillion-dollar level to assess periodically the achievement of Americans in reading, math, science, and other areas to determine growth over a period of years. In 1970 and 1971 the project tested over 98,000 9-, 13-, 17-, and 26- to 35-year-old individuals across the country to determine reading ability. The tests included such innovative, practical, and functional tasks as reading candy wrappers and cooking recipes. The results were dismal. Generally low reading ability was found across all age levels.[4] I was chosen to visit Denver with five other "reading experts" in September 1973 to help interpret the results of the NAEP. In addition to generally low achievement in reading across the board, the findings revealed that blacks, on the average, consistently scored lower than whites in almost every area of the tests. The logical conclusion from these data and similar studies is that blacks and other disadvantaged minorities are not taught to read as well as their white counterparts in schools (see Chap. 6). The report of our "reading specialist" meeting in Denver recommended improvements in teacher training, training more male elementary teachers, effective teaching of skills, and reexamining teacher attitudes toward minorities.[5] In a nationwide follow-up study in 1975, the NAEP found that 9-year-olds were reading better than their counterparts in 1971. The older children, however, were not.

Even among the elite group of students who graduate from high school and go on to college, reading ability seems to be declining. The Modern Language Association recently conducted a survey of the heads of English departments in colleges across the country and found widespread concern that "students are coming from high school with far less firm grasp on fundamentals than before—middle class as well as disadvantaged students."[6] The fastest-growing need on college campuses, in both 4-year colleges and 2-year junior and community colleges, is for reading-study specialists and programs to work with students with marginal reading skills.

Unfortunately, remedial programs at the elementary and college levels have not improved reading achievement. Sporadic crash programs such as the federal Title I and "Right to Read" programs have not produced widespread improvement of reading ability, especially in urban areas. Despite the wealth of information and data on the topic of reading, the only accepted conclusion is that the job is not being done well. There is considerable disagreement about why schools are failing in their primary responsibility. It follows that if we can really understand the reasons for the failure—given the fact that the failure is not total (most kids do learn to read)—we will then know what to do.

At a conservative estimate there are at least 18 million illiterate Americans.[7] We can only guess the true number of illiterate students who are dropping out or graduating from high schools every year. There is no accepted definition of functional literacy with which all Americans would agree. Many associate the word "literacy" with writing ability alone. If we defined functional literacy as the ability to read and write well enough to cope with the requirements for more than bare survival in our society—that is, the ability to read well enough to pass a driver's license examination, write well enough to fill out applications for Medicare and welfare, read warning signs (danger, poison, harmful, caution), and read a newspaper—then I suspect our number of illiterates is between 50 and 75 million Americans.

The fuzzy nature of statistical studies on literacy and the fact that schools generally do not release literacy data on state and national levels leave us good reason to be confused. But the general message certainly is that the schools are doing a poor job teaching reading.

The history of controversies over the teaching of reading is written of at length in other publications. Nila Smith,[8] Harold Lamport,[9] Charles Fries,[10] Jeanne Chall,[11] and Donald Gallo[12] have documented the data on and criticisms of reading instruction in the United

States. Perhaps the most comprehensive history is Nila Smith's 1965 update of a book originally published in 1934, *American Reading Instruction*.[13] Smith documented eight periods of changing emphasis in reading instruction from 1607 to 1965. The periods that closely parallel the social history of the United States, were, in order:[14]

- Religious Emphasis (1607–1776)
- Nationalistic-Moralistic (1776–1840)
- Education for Citizenship (1840–1890)
- Reading as a Cultural Asset (1890–1910)
- Scientific Investigation (1910–1925)
- Intensive Research and Application (1925–1935)
- International Conflict (1935–1950)
- Expanding Knowledge and Technological Revolution (1950–1965)

Debates over why children fail in reading ranged through the years over such issues as:

- whole word versus phonics emphasis in teaching beginning reading
- linguistic proposals for changing methods
- alphabet reformers' arguments to change the irregular spelling of the language
- which set of materials resulted in higher reading achievement
- how teachers should be certified as teachers and reading specialists
- whether reading is learning to read, or the process of reading content
- emotional problems
- physical lesions in the brain
- direct teaching versus discovery of reading
- readiness for reading or when reading instruction should begin
- the values of silent versus oral reading
- conflicting methodologies for treating reading disabilities
- definitions of reading
- speed reading
- the usefulness of reading machines
- learning disabilities

The reader who is interested in a detailed account should read one or more of the previously mentioned books.

The 1907 comment of Edmund Huey, noted educational psychologist of his time, is as relevant today as it was then:

A survey of the views of some of our foremost and soundest educators reveals the fact that the men of our time who are most competent to judge are profoundly dissatisfied with reading as it is carried on in the elementary schools.[15]

If one were to characterize the period from 1965 to 1978, it would have to be called the period of Questioning, Uncertainty, and Change. Criticisms of reading instruction over the past few years have come from reading professionals as well as laypersons. At no time in our history have so many books been written directly criticizing education. Most of these authors criticize the schools in general but use reading instruction in the schools as a focal point. For example, in *The Lives of Children*,[16] George Dennison describes a young Puerto Rican boy named José. José spends his evenings reading letters from Puerto Rico to his father, an illiterate, but he is unable to learn to read English in a public school and is labeled as a child with a learning disability. Mr. Dennison teaches the boy to read in an alternative school that treats José decently and with respect. The point is made that José does not have a "reading problem"; he has a "people problem" with the public school teachers. The major theme in most of the recent "popular" books about education is that schools and reading classes are inhumane and joyless and are staffed with incompetent, often prejudiced people.

The major argument over the years about reading has been over whether to emphasize phonics instruction or whole-word instruction and whether to emphasize skills or meaning (comprehension). Many people assume erroneously that phonics and sight words are two mutually exclusive methods of teaching reading. Actually, because of the irregularity of our written language, both methods have to be, and are, used in elementary schools. The real issue is the emphasis given to phonics, or code-breaking skills, versus that given to studying whole words and meaning. Likewise, authors argue over which method and materials to introduce first in a beginning reading program.

Sometimes, however, personal self-interest gets in the way of professional objectivity, especially when dealing with a topic as volatile as reading. On the other hand, some nonprofessionals have shown a remarkable perceptiveness of and sensitivity to some of the major problems with reading instruction.

Rudolf Flesch, the author of several books on "how to" speak, write, and think, wrote the only best-seller about reading instruction. His *Why Johnny Can't Read — And What You Can Do About It*[17] had a major impact on the reading world. The author was not considered a reading professional, and he certainly did not place himself among the ranks of reading "experts," but *Why Johnny Can't Read* was on *The New York Times* best-seller list for 37 weeks from April to December of 1955.

Flesch's book angrily criticized the "word method" of teaching reading. In this technique, used in many children's graded readers, children simultaneously associate the whole word with its sound and meaning. Whether called the "look-say," the "whole-word," the "synthetic," or the "meaning-first" method, this approach is popular today in initial reading instruction. The rationale is that if children can recognize a few words and their meanings "at sight," or instantly, they will experience "reading." "Experience charts" are used to facilitate learning these "sight words." A typical experience chart after the children take a walk in the woods may look like this on the classroom blackboard:

Our Walk
We went for a walk.
We saw a pond.
We saw a duck.
Sally hurt her leg.

The children actually write the story with the teacher, using their own words. Then they are able to read the words "at sight."

Unlike speech, reading is not a natural process for children; however, they are usually highly motivated to learn to read. The experience chart sustains this interest and causes children to believe they are reading. Shortly after they learn a reasonable number of sight words through writing stories about things and situations they are familiar with, they are usually started on the tedious road of learning the sound-symbol or letter-sound correspondences in our language with all its spelling and pronunciation irregularities.*

Flesch, writing in 1955, believed that phonics or sound-letter relationships were not being emphasized in the teaching of reading. His attack quoted everyone from Lee Cronbach,[20] still a very respected statistician, to Donald Agnew, author in 1939 of a research study that is often cited as an example of the worst in research technology.[21] Flesch's impassioned plea for the teaching of phonics attacked the leaders in the reading field at the time (William Gray, Arthur Gates, Donald Durrell, Paul Witty, and others) for advocating the use of basal readers which emphasized whole-word teaching over phonics. He let his emotional

---

*Using computers, researchers have studied some of the old rules we used to learn in school about spelling and pronunciation and have discovered that many such rules actually applied to only about half the words.[18] For example, in one study,[19] Ted Clymer analyzed 686 words having two vowels together ("when two vowels go walking, the first one does the talking" or "when two vowels are together in a word, the first vowel has a long sound") and found that in 377, or 45 percent of the words, the first vowel did not have its long sound (i.e., *found, sound, bear*).

appeal in favor of phonics (that is, stating that the English language is 90 percent phonetic) go too far, and his book was discounted among reading professionals as the work of a crank.

The book was angrily attacked by schoolteachers and reading professionals and just as angrily defended by aroused parents who bought millions of copies. It was syndicated in newspapers throughout the country and was the basis of articles in several national magazines in the summer of 1955.[22] Yet, in the most comprehensive history of reading instruction by a reading professional, Nila Smith's *American Reading Instruction* of 1965, absolutely no mention was made of *Why Johnny Can't Read*.

It is interesting to look at some of the remarks of reading professionals who did react to Flesch's book. Emmett Betts, then psychology professor at Temple University, director of the Temple Reading Clinic, and author of a widely used textbook[23] on how to teach reading, called Flesch "a master of histrionics." He accused Flesch of twisting definitions.[24] Helen Robinson, who was the "William S. Gray" Professor of Reading at the University of Chicago (William S. Gray was the original author of the Scott-Foresman "Dick and Jane" readers) called Flesch's implication that there was a conspiracy among publishers, reading specialists, and universities to avoid teaching letters and sounds "ridiculous and . . . typical of the generalizations made on the basis of limited experience."[25] John De Boer, another reading-textbook author, said that Flesch was writing outside his field of competence, that his treatment of learning was "bizarre," and that "bobbles" could be found on any page.[26]

Many of the reactions to Flesch's book were clearly for protection of self-interest. The late Arthur Gates's responses to attacks on basal readers offer one illustration. For many years an influential reading expert at Columbia University, Gates responded in articles entitled "A Review of Rudolf Flesch, *Why Johnny Can't Read*"[27] and "The Teaching of Reading—Objective Evidence Versus Opinion."[28]

Gates first attacked Flesch's book. In an 18-page booklet published by his basal-reader-series publisher, Macmillan, he attempted to break down Flesch's attack point by point. Gates had been personally mentioned in the book along with other authorities, and his anger was understandable. His other response was to two books published in 1961, *What Ivan Knows that Johnny Doesn't*[29] and *Tomorrow's Illiterates: The State of Reading Instruction Today*.[30] Both books were attacks on reading instruction and basal readers in particular, reflecting an interest in learning to read for national survival immediately following Russia's launching of *Sputnik*. In defending basal readers (the graded books used in 95 percent of the schools in the United States as the major component of the reading program), Gates stated that, "In the new program the basal reader is devoted frankly to the task of teaching the abilities and skills needed to read well and enjoy it."[31] Then in the very next paragraph, he cited evidence that "basal readers are more likely to frustrate than encourage the enjoyment of reading." Of course, Gates had to defend basal readers, for he was the major author of a very lucrative set of readers—*The Macmillan Readers.*

I could not find a positive review of the Flesch book written by a reading professional. However, the *Saturday Review* reported that it "may well be ranked the most important contribution to the betterment of public-school teaching methods in the past two decades."[32] The *Chicago Sunday Tribune* stated, "If the 'word method' experts can meet Flesch's challenge, they should do it. Parents want clear, honest answers. They will not be put off with 'teacher knows best'."[33]

Flesch was clearly in favor of a phonics emphasis in teaching reading, and he made some important contributions to the field. He suggested a cartel-like relationship between publishers, reading specialists, and university professors. He made parents aware that children were not learning to read, regardless of what the teaching approach was, and he caused reading personnel to reevaluate *their* thinking and methodology and to become concerned about achievement in reading.*

In 1967, Jeanne Chall, a recognized reading expert, professor, and director of the reading program at Harvard University, published a study of reading funded by the Carnegie Foundation, *Learning to Read: The Great Debate.*[35] Her purpose was to analyze existing research objectively, comparing different methods of teaching beginning reading. Her work was a comprehensive documentation of materials, methods, and techniques of teaching reading, including interviews with teachers and administrators as well as reports of research studies. She concluded that an emphasis on breaking the code or phonics "produces better results, at least up to the point where sufficient evidence seems to be available, the end of third grade."[36] Chall clearly did not agree with Flesch, however. Flesch devoted his whole book to the teaching of phonics. Chall devoted less than a paragraph to the notion that a phonics emphasis seems to produce better results.

Her book was scholarly; Flesch's appealed to a popular audience. Chall qualified her statements to insure that her views were clearly understood, but, since she dared to question established practices, her book, like Flesch's, was not readily accepted by the reading

---

*In February 1975, a New York librarian suggested that a mother read the 20-year-old book. The mother took her 6 year old out of school as a result and started teaching him herself using Flesch's suggestions—phonics. The school board charged the mother with child neglect,[34] and the Flesch controversy came alive again.

profession. The reactions of George Spache and Leo Fay and Ruth Strang (all reading professionals) were typical among those who felt the basal readers were threatened. Spache stated that the book served "to buttress Chall's own concept of the proper phonics approach under the cloak of what is supposed to be a comprehensive and dispassionate review of the related research."[37] Fay and Strang found Chall's book to be more "confusing" than clarifying.[38]

I read Chall's book when I was working for a year in the U.S. Office of Education. I happened to be riding on an elevator with Harold Howe, then U.S. commissioner of education, when he was taking Chall's book to John Gardner, then secretary of the Department of Health, Education and Welfare (HEW). Howe said "This is the first book about reading that has made any sense to me. Now I know what all the fuss is about."[39] Dr. Chall was invited to consult with the Office of Education on several reading projects as a result of her book.

Both Flesch's and Chall's books threatened the professional reading establishment. They clearly helped swing the pendulum in the phonics/look-say debate back toward a phonics emphasis.

As long as some basal readers emphasize the sight method first, and teach phonics later, and as long as phonics-oriented approaches emphasize decoding first, and later teach children to recognize irregularly spelled words on sight, there will be controversy over which approach is better. Indeed, there are over 100 approaches to teaching beginning reading,[40] and one could argue endlessly over the virtues of any one of them. Shortly before Chall's book was published, the data began to come in on a large-scale research effort of the U.S. Office of Education, "The First Grade Studies."[41] Twenty-seven universities across the country spent 1 million dollars of federal money to compare several different representative approaches to beginning reading instruction. The conclusion: there is no one best way to teach reading, but the teacher does make a difference.[42]

Every few years a "panacea" is discovered and advertised with great hoopla in the popular press. In the 1960s there were five such examples of fairly radical innovations in beginning reading instruction; all five were hailed in the popular press as promising new and exciting ways of teaching beginning reading:

1. In 1962, Caleb Gattegno introduced *Words in Color,*[43] which was based on a chart which had all the letters of the alphabet color coded. The approach was used in very few schools, but the author's salesmanship abilities kept the approach in the public eye.

2. In 1963, Glenn Doman, a physical therapist, appealed to young mothers of the country with *How to Teach Your Baby to Read.*[44] The book advertised a widely discredited "patterning" approach to remediating reading problems.[45,46] Doman also recommended using

large cards with words on them for a few minutes each day (teaching words at sight).

3. Also in 1963, i.t.a.[47] was brought to this country from England. Sir James Pitman's phonetic alphabet, the "Initial Teaching Alphabet," was designed to regularize our alphabet so that there would be a direct relationship between sound and symbol in all words. Some 40 symbols were presented to replace the 26 traditional letters. Children learned to read in i.t.a. and then were gradually transferred to the regular alphabet.

4. In 1964, the concept of "linguistic readers" was introduced. Charles Fries, a noted linguist at the University of Michigan, with Rosemary Wilson, a Philadelphia reading specialist, published a set of linguistically oriented readers called the *Merrill Linguistic Readers*.[48] The application of "linguistic principles" to the teaching of reading caught on and several other publishers introduced "linguistic" versions of their basal reader series. However, there was great confusion over what "linguistic principles" were being followed in developing the linguistic readers. In the early 1960s teachers flocked to courses on linguistics at local colleges to understand these new linguistic principles used in the readers. Unfortunately, some courses were taught by linguistic professors who knew no linguistics beyond the history of language and articulatory phonetics (how speech sounds are made) let alone anything about reading instruction. For example, one important linguistic principle is that speech is primary. It would follow that children should learn to read the same language or dialect that they speak. Given the hundreds of regional and social variations in dialect in this country, one would expect school readers which are "linguistically" oriented to reflect this.

5. *Distar*,[49] discussed at length in Chap. 6, appeared in published form in 1972 but was widely distributed by its authors in mimeographed form from about 1968. It is a good example of a phonics-emphasis approach rooted firmly in behavioristic psychology. It emphasizes the Skinnerian approach of rewarding correct responses with candy or tokens, which can be used to "buy" other rewards, the same way Dr. Skinner trains pigeons at Harvard. Some of the "linguistic" approaches also used the term "programmed" to describe a series of "rewards" for each correct answer.

Words in Color was used in many federally funded programs; Doman's work was a forerunner to the "early teaching of reading" movement; i.t.a. was used in schools in practically every state of the union; linguistic readers were used in at least 75 percent of the states; and *Distar* was very popular in some federal programs. But where are they now? All five have faded in popularity, and one would be hard pressed to find more than a few school systems that advocate the use of these materials.

A new crop of reading approaches appears each year. One in current favor is *Alpha One*,[50] an extremely sexist approach when first published. Once this was discovered by the feminist movement, *Alpha One* was revised (the vowels were all female and the consonants male). New approaches to teaching reading will continue to appear, and they will continue to be accepted as possible solutions to the causes of illiteracy. But new sets of materials and the attendant teacher enthusiasm quickly succumb to the reality that materials don't teach reading, teachers do.

In 1964, while I was in graduate school at the University of Pennsylvania, I worked with Ralph Preston, director of the University Reading Clinic. The clinic performs diagnostic case studies and provides remedial tutoring for children with relatively serious reading problems. After working there for several months, I wondered what happened to these kids 5 or 10 years later. Since the clinic had been in operation for a number of years and kept very detailed records, I decided to check out my hypothesis that having early reading problems really doesn't cripple one for life. I attempted to contact 96 individuals who had attended the reading clinic 8 years earlier with severe reading problems. I was able to reach 50 of them by telephone. I interviewed either the client or a parent, asking questions about the educational level attained and current employment. The group of 50 children were of average ability and, other than the fact that they had had reading disabilities, compared favorably with any average group of American children. The rate of unemployment in this group was not significantly different from the national population. In comparing my data with data on the general population, I found that the 50 children fulfilled educational and vocational roles comparable to those fulfilled by others of their age in the general population. The percentage enrolled in high school and their rate of success in graduating from high school conformed to the national rates. Almost as high a proportion of the group gained admission to college as in the general population.[51]

I submit that if follow-up studies were to be done on children who have reading problems now, they would produce the same results. It is interesting to note that my follow-up study covered a period between 1955 and 1963. This was a period during which little change took place in American education, a period during which schools were bound to "book learning."*

---

*A number of well-known men had severe reading problems as school-children. Among them are Thomas Edison, Harvey Cushing, Woodrow Wilson, Auguste Rodin, Albert Einstein, Paul Ehrlich, and George S. Patton IV.[52]

After so much controversy and so many efforts to improve the teaching of reading, we might be led to believe that the problem of illiteracy is subsiding, that the teaching of reading is improving. It isn't. With the completion of "The First Grade Studies," emphasis on methods and materials should have shifted to an examination of teachers and schools. This occurred to a certain extent. Congress insists on an accounting of how federal money for education is being spent, and there is a new emphasis on delineating specific objectives for teaching reading, on teacher training innovations, and on continuing the search for the secret of how children learn to read, although as yet there have been no dramatic breakthroughs in teacher training, or in discovering how children learn to read, or in instructional practices resulting in better achievement in reading.

The real problem—the reason there doesn't seem to be a single solution—is the institution I call The Great American Reading Machine. It is easy to lay the blame with the kids themselves, or the methods, or teacher training, or lack of money, or the teachers, or the materials. I would suggest that all are to blame and none are to blame. What has not been questioned is all the mechanisms, agencies, people, organizations, and other influences that directly and indirectly influence the teaching of reading in each child's classroom. That structure or institution is The Great American Reading Machine. The following chapters describe its complexity and its effect on children.

References

1. Allen, James E., Jr., "The Right to Read—Target for the 70's," speech delivered before the Annual Convention of the National Association of State Boards of Education, Century Plaza Hotel, Los Angeles, Calif., September 23, 1969, distributed by the U.S. Department of Health, Education and Welfare.
2. Harris, Louis and Associates, Inc., *Survival Literacy Study,* No. 2036, conducted for the National Reading Council, September 1970, 39 p. (mimeographed).
3. U.S. Department of Commerce, Bureau of the Census, *1970 Census of Population,* "Population and Housing Characteristics for the United States, by State: 1970," "Social Characteristics of the Population: 1970," PC (SI)-29, December 1972.
4. National Assessment of Educational Progress, Reading Reports, Nos. 02-GIY, 02-R-09, 02-R-08, 02-R-03, 02-R-05, 02-R-20, 02-R-02, 02-R-06, 02-R-04, 02-R-07, Supt. of Documents, U.S. Government Printing Office, Washington, D.C., 1972–1973.
5. Gallo, Donald, *Recipes, Wrappers, Reasoning and Rate: A Digest of the First Reading Assessment,* National Assessment of Educational Progress, Supt.

of Documents, U.S. Government Printing Office, Washington, D.C., 1974.

6. Scully, Malcolm G., "Crisis in English Writing," *The Chronicle of Higher Education,* vol, IX, No. 1, September 23, 1974, p. 1.

7. Harris, Louis and Associates, Inc., *loc. cit.*

8. Smith, Nila B., *American Reading Instruction,* International Reading Association, Newark, Del. 1965 edition.

9. Lamport, Harold B., "A History of the Teaching of Beginning Reading," unpublished doctoral dissertation, University of Chicago, 1935, pp. 487–516.

10. Fries, Charles C., *Linguistics and Reading,* Holt, Rinehart and Winston, Inc., New York, 1962, pp. 1–34

11. Chall, Jeanne S., *Learning to Read: The Great Debate,* McGraw-Hill Book Co., New York, 1967, pp. 13–74.

12. Gallo, Donald, *op. cit.*

13. Smith, Nila B., *A Historical Analysis of American Reading Instruction,* Silver Burdett and Co., Morristown, N.J., 1934 edition.

14. Smith, Nila B., *American Reading Instruction,* pp. 427–439.

15. Huey, Edmund B., *The Psychology and Pedagogy of Reading,* Macmillan Co., New York, 1908, p. 301.

16. Dennison, George, *The Lives of Children,* Random House, New York, 1969.

17. Flesch, Rudolf, *Why Johnny Can't Read—And What You Can Do About It,* Harper & Row, New York, 1955.

18. Burmeister, Lou E., "Usefulness of Phonic Generalizations," *The Reading Teacher,* vol. 21, January 1968, pp. 349–256.

19. Clymer, Ted, "The Utility of Phonic Generalizations in the Primary Grades," *The Reading Teacher,* vol. 16, January 1963, pp. 252–258.

20. Flesch, Rudolph, *op. cit.,* p. 44.

21. Agnew, Donald C., *Effect of Varied Amounts of Phonic Training on Primary Reading,* Duke University Press, Durham, N.C., 1939.

22. Betts, Emmett A., "Teaching Johnny to Read," *Saturday Review,* vol. 38, No. 20, July 30, 1955, p. 20.

23. Betts, Emmett A., *Foundations of Reading Instruction,* American Book Co., New York, 1950.

24. Betts, Emmett A., "Teaching Johnny to Read," *op. cit.,* p. 21.

25. Robinson, Helen M., "Reviews," *Elementary School Journal,* vol. 56, October 1955, p. 91.

26. De Boer, John J., "Flesch on Reading—An Editorial," *Elementary English,* vol. 32, April 1955, pp. 199–200.

27. Gates, Arthur, "A Review of Rudolf Flesch, *Why Johnny Can't Read,*" Macmillan Co., New York, circa 1955, undated.

28. Gates, Arthur, "The Teaching of Reading—Objective Evidence Versus Opinion," *Phi Delta Kappan,* vol. 53, No. 6, February 1962, pp. 197–205.

29. Trace, Arthur S., Jr., *What Ivan Knows that Johnny Doesn't,* Random House, New York, 1961.

30. Walcutt, Charles (editor), *Tomorrow's Illiterates: The State of Reading Instruction Today,* Counsel for Basic Education, Little, Brown and Co., Boston, 1961.

31. Gates, Arthur, "The Teaching of Reading—Objective Evidence Versus Opinion," *op. cit.,* p. 203.

32. Morris, William, "Teaching Johnny to Read," *Saturday Review,* vol. 38, No. 20, July 30, 1955, p. 21.

33. Stockwell, La Tourette, *Chicago Sunday Tribune,* March 13, 1955, p. 4.

34. "Mom Outteaches School, Is Charged with Neglect," New York, Associated Press release, *Grand Rapids Press,* February 20, 1975.

35. Chall, Jeanne, *Learning to Read: The Great Debate,* McGraw-Hill Book Co., New York, 1967.

36. Chall, Jeanne, *op. cit.,* p. 307.

37. Spache, George, "Review, *Learning to Read: The Great Debate,*" *Journal of Reading Behavior,* vol. 1, Winter 1969, pp. 71–74.

38. Fay, Leo, and Strang, Ruth, "Review, *Learning to Read: The Great Debate,*" *The Reading Teacher,* vol. 21, March 1968, p. 575.

39. Howe, Harold, conversation, February 3, 1968.

40. Aukerman, Robert, *Approaches to Beginning Reading,* John Wiley & Sons, Inc., New York, 1971.

41. *The Reading Teacher,* vol. 19, No. 8, May 1966, and vol. 20, No. 1, October 1966, entire issues.

42. "It is likely that improvement in reading instruction can be brought about more efficiently by improved selection and training of teachers, by improved in-service training programs, and by improved school learning climates than by instituting changes in instructional materials." From Dykstra, Robert, "Classroom Implications of the First-Grade Studies," in *Professional Focus on Reading* (Proceedings of the College Reading Association Conference), edited by Clay Ketcham, vol. 9, 1968, pp. 53–59.

43. Gattegno, Caleb, *Words in Color,* Teacher's Guide, Learning Materials, Inc., Chicago, 1962.

44. Doman, Glenn, *How to Teach Your Baby to Read, The Gentle Revolution,* Random House, New York, 1963.

45. Robbins, Melvyn Paul, "The Delacato Interpretation of Neurological Organization," *Reading Research Quarterly,* Spring 1966, vol. 1, No. 3, pp. 57–78.

46. Whitsell, Leon J., "Delacato's Neurological Organization, a Medical Appraisal," *California School Health,* Fall 1967, vol. 3, No. 3, pp. 1–3.

47. Tanyzer, Harold "The Nature and Functions of i.t.a. in Beginning Reading," in *A Decade of Innovations: Approaches to Beginning Reading,*

edited by Elaine Vilscek, International Reading Association, Newark, Del. 1968, p. 121.

48. Wilson, Rosemary G., *"A Linguistic Approach to Beginning Reading Based on Fries' Principle,"* in *Improvement of Reading through Classroom Practice,* in Ninth International Reading Association Conference Proceedings, 1964, p. 225.

49. Englemann, Siegfried, and Stearns, Susan, *Distar,* Science Research Associates Inc., Chicago, 1972.

50. *Alpha One,* New Dimensions in Education, Inc., Jericho, N.Y., 1968.

51. Preston, Ralph C., and Yarington, David J., "Status of Fifty Retarded Readers Eight Years after Clinical Diagnosis," *Journal of Reading,* vol. 12, November 1967, pp. 122–129.

52. Thompson, Lloyd J., "Language Disabilities in Men of Eminence," *Journal of Learning Disabilities,* vol. 4, January 1971, pp. 34–45.

TWO

THE GREAT AMERICAN READING MACHINE

I use the term The Great American Reading Machine as a metaphor to represent the complex interrelationships between and among the federal government, state education departments, local school boards, local school administrators, reading specialists, classroom teachers, professional organizations, professors of education, the press, authors of school readers, publishers, and foundations. The ultimate result of the various interrelationships is what happens in schools when children are taught reading.

The Great American Reading Machine is not a tight institution with clearly observable boundaries like the American Bar Association or the American Medical Association with their review boards, certifying procedures, and organizational structures. But The Great American Reading Machine ultimately affects every child in every school; it causes the illiteracy problem in the United States. It is a complex contraption that feeds upon itself: it is self-perpetuating, inbred, and self-supporting. It is like "The House that Jack Built":

1. Professors of education write the readers that professors of education train teachers to use in school.
2. Local school administrators get advanced degrees with professors of education, who consult with and advise school boards, who buy school readers written by professors of education.
3. The federal government and foundations pay millions of dollars to state education departments, colleges, and school boards to pay salaries to professors of education, reading specialists, and local administrators.
4. Reading specialists, teachers, local administrators, and school board members read textbooks, journal articles, and research reports written by professors of education.
5. Publishing companies are paid by federal, state, and local funds to provide materials written by professors of education and reading specialists.

6. All the members belong to professional organizations which have annual meetings to facilitate the flow of money and influence between and among them.

The best graphic description of the Machine I can provide is the drawing below illustrating the flow of both money and influence. The Great American Reading Machine is a stable social institution in which leadership is controlled and limited to proven followers of the creed for the protection of the organization. As an institution, it determines the quality of the teaching of reading to children. It is an institution that is so established that it has withstood continued criticism from within and without for 200 years. The reasons it has remained

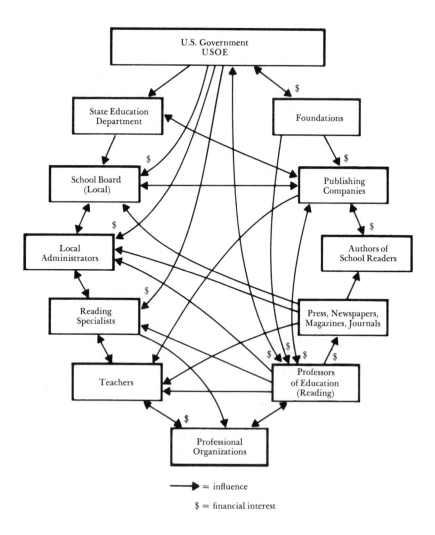

⟶ = influence

$ = financial interest

intact are the bureaucracy, tradition, the "people problem," and inertia. Following is a discussion of each.

Bureaucracy. The institution is one that has produced such large
programs, positions, and influence that to tear it down completely
would be to destroy the entire public school system in the country.
Some have suggested just that,[1] but no viable alternatives have been
offered. During the 1960s and early 1970s the federal government
poured so many millions of dollars directly and peripherally into
reading instruction that a bureaucracy of reading personnel has been
built up and tenured (after 3 years of teaching, teachers are almost
automatically given this life-contract under which they can be fired
only for gross negligence or moral turpitude). And the same thing has
happened at the college and university level. Reading teachers and
university reading professors, the people who directly operate The
Great American Reading Machine, *are* bureaucrats in the sense that
they endeavor to preserve their empires, however small, and to run
them with a minimum of disruption. Any change is perceived as a
threat, and they will cling to traditional practices to protect themselves
and their positions.

Tradition. There is no doubt that The Great American Reading
Machine is a traditional social system and that tradition is the most
powerful form of social inertia. Grade levels in reading, readability
levels of books, censorship, reading remediation, speed reading, seeing
television as a threat, reading methods, reading teachers being equal,
books teaching reading, reading tests, every teacher being a reading
teacher, and the hidden curricula of reading are concepts which are
questioned rarely, but they are in this book.

People problem. Nevitt Sanford, a well-known leader in higher-
education research, has described deterrents to change in higher education as a "people problem." Sanford described college faculties as
being a major conservative force deterring change.

> In order to resist pressures from outside, as well as to further
> their most immediate interests, faculties have fostered an in-
> group spirit, built up traditions of faculty prerogatives, in-
> stalled the machinery of campus democracy. These are the
> very things that now make change very difficult, even when the
> impulse to change arises largely from within the faculty itself.
> . . . Faculties sometimes go so far in protecting their profes-
> sional status, or in using their professional status to satisfy their
> desires for security, and the advancement of their own inter-
> ests, that they neglect the legitimate needs and aspirations of
> the society that supports higher learning.[2]

Elementary and secondary school teachers are no less protective. Notice the great rise in influence of the teachers' unions. The unions have successfully raised teachers' salaries to an acceptable level, but at the same time successful lobbying power plays and negotiations have given teachers the power to protect the status quo as well as their jobs. In some ways, schools have imitated the industrial revolution. We often mourn the loss of the craftsmanship of the old furniture and house builders. But we expect our teachers to be the individual caring craftsmen of the past. They are not. They are basically good, well-meaning individuals, but they are caught up in the Machine. Teachers' unions, boring teacher training programs, lack of jobs, fear of parent pressures, and low salaries have forced teachers to join the ever more powerful unions, which just add another cog to the Machine.

Inertia. The last major reason the institution of The Great American Reading Machine is unwilling to change is inertia. Taxpayers continue to support it even though it does its job badly. There is no convincing data available on how children learn to read, nor, for that matter, on how children learn, although we can and do espouse theories. We can physically describe the movements of the eyes, and we can describe the results of reading, that is, comprehension of materials read. But we have no real scientific basis for what we do in teaching reading. That is why materials and techniques for doing the job have proliferated. Methods, materials, or techniques that work for one child are often assumed to work for another. Because there are no scientific bases for teaching reading, "experts" abound. The schools end up promising more than they can deliver, yet they deliver enough to have kept parents relatively happy for 200 years: taxpayers have supported compulsory public education for many, many years with very few questions asked.

The Great American Reading Machine is so complicated, so interrelated among schools, universities, federal agencies, publishers, commercial suppliers of materials other than books, and the various interests of people in diverse and unfortunately often antagonistic roles—from company presidents to school board members to researchers—that it is impossible to blame the failure of children to learn to read directly on the human beings who teach children, or on the school system the children attend. It is much more complicated than that. It's not the teacher's fault, it's not the principal's fault, it's not the school board's fault; they are the way they are because of the larger institution which has molded them, conditioned them to behave the way they do. It is a huge swirling cycle, made up of small swirling cycles continually reproducing themselves like slow-motion tornadoes, whose outcome is a large number of illiterate children every year.

One example of one of the cycles is the following: Ms. A., an elementary teacher, goes to X College to work on her reading-specialist certification, where Dr. Z. is her professor in Education 902, "How to Teach Reading." Dr. Z. has received a research grant from the U.S. Office of Education to develop materials for teaching beginning reading. Ms. A. tries out the materials while in Dr. Z.'s class and is taught that this technique is the best. When the grant ends, Publisher S. publishes the materials and Ms. A., now a reading specialist, recommends that her school system buy them for all the schools. For the next 20 years, every teacher graduating from X College recommends the materials to his or her school system. Some of the teachers are promoted and become reading specialists; some go back to graduate school and become professors. At professional meetings and in the professional journals they talk and write about the materials. The materials are adopted by the state education department because they are so popular. Dr. Z. retires to a mansion and summers in Europe. The publishing company gives raises to its salespeople. The teachers and professors advance in the profession.

Now, one may ask, what's wrong with all that if the materials work, if the kids learn to read? Nothing, but one look at the box score on how the Machine has done over the years shows us that The Great American Reading Machine strikes out all too often.

Carl Rogers, a psychologist and a leader in the movement to "humanize" the schools, asks a very important question in his book on teaching, *Freedom to Learn*.[3] What he says about education in general can be applied to the Machine:

> Can the educational system as a whole, the most traditional, conservative, rigid, bureaucratic institution of our time (and I use these words descriptively rather than cynically) come to grips with the real problems of modern life? Or will it continue to be shackled by the tremendous social pressures for conformity and retrogression, added to its own traditionalism?

What is the solution to the problem? Will it be solved by iconoclasts, radical parents, and enlightened teachers writing and talking about it? I doubt it. One strategy for change is all-out rejection of the traditional practices in teaching reading. Teachers could be encouraged to do their own thing. "Try out anything new; it can't be any worse than the old way." This theory holds that when the call comes to return to normal, which certainly would be soon, the schools would have been so shaken that "normal" would be much different and hopefully better than teaching was initially. Another theory holds that leaders cause changes. Leaders who recognize that changes are needed in the traditional practices call for these changes and the membership follows along as directed. Other possible change agents are radical innovators who capture the attention of the financiers of reading education. With all the money so placed with the innovations, the teachers and schools change for financial survival.

However, these strategies for change are unlikely to result in lasting increased achievement in reading and the ultimate eradication of illiteracy. They would more likely result in controversy, in taking sides, and perhaps most damaging, in pulling apart the modest unity that does exist between reading educators and parents. Congress has passed a National Reading Improvement Program[4] to provide financial assistance to improve the teaching of reading. Part C of the law provides for reading specialists to take over the job of teaching reading in grades 1 and 2. Congress as yet has not appropriated any money to carry out the intention of the law, but if it does, I would predict that it would have the effect of the above strategies.

The first step, it seems to me, in any move toward improvement of reading achievement in this country, is recognizing that a problem exists and understanding the nature and complexities of the cause.

References

1. Illich, Ivan, *Deschooling Society,* Harper & Row, New York, 1970.
2. Sanford, Nevitt, "Higher Education as a Social Pattern," in *The American College,* edited by Nevitt Sanford, John Wiley & Sons, Inc., New York, 1962, p. 21.
3. Rogers, Carl, *Freedom to Learn,* Charles E. Merrill Publishing Co., Columbus, Ohio, 1969, p. vii.
4. Public Law 93-380, Title VII, 1975.

THREE

GOVERNMENT

Probably the most influential cogs in The Great American Reading Machine are federal, state, and local government educational agencies.

At the federal level, the U.S. Office of Education (USOE), one of the largest components of the Department of Health, Education and Welfare (HEW), has over 3,000 employees administering and financing educational programs across the country. This agency, along with the new National Institute for Education (NIE), changes its focus with each new political administration because of new education legislation and new priorities. They fund educational research programs, innovative classroom techniques and programs, financial aid programs for colleges, educational programs for the children of poor families, school lunch programs, school and college curriculum development projects, and all other federal programs dealing with education. The most important contribution made by the federal government is financial. The USOE has spent an average of 5 billion dollars a year on education, much of it on reading programs.

We are lucky to live in a country where so much financial aid is given to education. This aid has helped thousands of children learn to read. Without the financial aid of the federal government, our illiteracy rate would surely be higher. But federal funding of reading programs is not without problems. Congresswoman Edith Green discovered in 1972, in her careful review of the USOE, that 90 percent of the contracts and grants awarded were given out on a noncompetitive basis. She said we are "witnessing the rise of an education–poverty–industrial complex in which the federal bureaucracies are able to dispense hundreds of millions of dollars in deals that are close to arrangements between friends."[1] The essential questions are: Have these federal dollars been influential in reducing illiteracy and are they paid to the appropriate people?

23

At the state level, each of the 50 states has an education department which, in addition to helping administer some of the federal programs, controls the licensing (certification) of teachers in the state and in some cases carries out the state government's wishes to control and mandate programs. For example, the state of Texas publishes a list of "approved" tests. School systems are not allowed to use state funds for textbooks that do not appear on the list. The state of Texas recently attempted unsuccessfully to mandate that all teacher-education colleges have similar training programs. The Texas college and public school personnel were so upset that they lobbied to have the law repealed on the grounds that it was unconstitutional. The state of Michigan has attempted to force an accountability model, which, if implemented, would eventually require that all teachers teach to the same objectives, which would have the effect of evaluating whether or not teachers are doing a good job. The teachers, so threatened, lobbied successfully, it appears, through their strong union, against such accountability measures.

State education departments in addition to monitoring educational programs in the state, also fund programs similar to those of the federal government, but on a smaller scale. The major share of state monies goes to supporting state colleges and universities. Some state education departments have built up huge bureaucracies and have tremendous influence over the public schools. The states of California and New York, for example, have more employees than does the USOE in Washington. Most state education departments can be characterized in the same manner as the USOE often is—as a group of people who easily get lost in the paper work and constraints of the bureaucracy and end up appearing to the people they serve as "inept" bureaucrats. For example, the USOE recently "found" several thousand dollars that had not been spent yet. Given their budget, several thousand dollars is not much money, but how often does this happen in how many government agencies?

Local educational government is usually administered by an elected or appointed school board. The school board collects local taxes and finances and administers the local school system (with the aid of state and federal monies). School boards have traditionally been staffed with local community leaders, doctors, lawyers, and interested mothers and fathers. These people have little time for the day-to-day running of the schools and are usually satisfied to concern themselves with budgetary matters and the few controversies that arise. But recently school boards have begun taking a more active role in administrative decisions, especially the large city boards of Chicago, New York, Los Angeles, and Philadelphia. They want more of a say in how the money is spent.

Governmental agencies have a powerful influence on schools and reading programs because they decide where and how the money will be spent. Government funding has never been "no-strings-attached" funding.

Let's look at some programs and procedures.

Federal Involvement in Reading

The USOE spends more money annually on education than any other government agency. Each year since the early 1960s it has spent millions of dollars on reading programs.[2] The USOE is careful to state that it does not control education. It does, however, set guidelines, priorities, and funding levels and funds programs and satisfies politicians. In other words, government money dictates the amount of emphasis on reading programs.

During the time I worked in the USOE, from September 1967 until June 1968, I learned much about the behind-the-scenes maneuverings and pressures that the following chronology of events from 1964 to the middle 1970s outlines.

1964. The USOE at this time had a Bureau of Research which administered the "Cooperative Research Program." A panel of outside "experts," the Research Advisory Council, made most of the important funding decisions for the bureau. Donald Durrell, a reading professor then at Boston University and a pillar of the reading establishment for many years, sat on the Research Advisory Council. In 1964 he persuaded the council to launch a large-scale effort to discover the best method of teaching reading. Over a million dollars was authorized to fund 14 university studies comparing methods of teaching beginning reading to 1st graders. Second graders were studied later. Eventually over 20,000 children were used in 27 different studies. No significant differences were found among the various reading programs. The major finding, it seems, was that if there were any differences among programs, they were teacher differences.[3] That is, the teacher makes the difference, not the program. The joke around the USOE thereafter was that it cost the agency more than 1 million dollars to get the members of the reading establishment to agree that there is no one best way to teach reading.

1965–1966. The passage of the Elementary and Secondary Education Act (ESEA), combined with the Economic Opportunity Act of 1965, poured massive funds into education. Most were eventually funneled into reading programs, since that seemed to be the area of greatest need. In 1965, school reading programs began their transformation from used Volkswagen sedans into new Cadillac convertibles. Funds became available for teacher training, new reading teachers, new reading programs, new books, and new hardware (recorders, machines, flashmeters, controlled readers, etc.). More than 1 billion dollars a year has been spent on reading-related projects since then. From 1964 to 1968, an average of more than 2 million dollars a year was spent on reading research alone.[4]

Reading was the top priority for most of the funds spent on schools with poor and "disadvantaged" pupils. Under Title I of ESEA, school systems with children in attendance from poor and disadvantaged families were eligible for large sums of money on a per-pupil basis. Administrators in these school systems, having no experience with writing proposals for federal funds or in spending large sums of money, were elated when their proposals were funded. Nearly all Title I proposals received by the USOE in 1965 and 1966 were funded regardless of content. The unsuspecting schools were bilked during those years by private enterprise, when reading machines, gadgets, packaged programs, and overhead projectors flooded the schools.

I was invited to visit a small school system in rural Appalachian Kentucky in 1966 to help them set up their reading program. In one school I was asked to show the teachers how to operate their new reading machine, for which they had paid $50,000. I was ushered into a room that contained a huge console of some 20 pairs of headsets attached to about five tape recorders. Boxes of tapes and pamphlets were spread about the room. The salesman had failed to return as promised to teach them how to use this remarkable new reading machine, paid for by the federal government's Title I program.

1967. President Johnson, a former teacher, had an interest in reading problems, because one of his children had had difficulty learning to read. He mentioned reading problems in almost every "poor people" speech, and directed John Gardner, then secretary of HEW, to establish a White House commission to study serious reading problems. At the same time that the Commission on Reading Problems was forming, Monte Penney, a research coordinator in the Bureau of Research of USOE, was organizing the "Targeted Reading Research Program." Using a new "convergence technique,"[5] Penney and his colleagues planned to chart what was known about reading and what needed to be learned about it into a 10-year plan for research that looked like the schedule for a huge tennis tournament. Penney managed to fund a few projects before the money ran out. Most notable of these was a large-scale research review edited by one of the most respected reading researchers in the country, the late Frederick B. Davis, of the University of Pennsylvania.

Penney recognized that all our knowledge about reading was based on theories, not facts, and that we had very little knowledge about the reading act itself. He was on the right track.

1968. At the time President Johnson directed the formation of a White House Commission on Reading, Congress was asking him to cut 6 billion dollars from his budget. This was not the time for him to launch a new White House effort. He directed Secretary Gardner of HEW to name a "National Advisory Committee on Dyslexia and Related Reading Disorders." Dyslexia was a catch-all term for reading problems and had myriad definitions.

As mentioned in Chap. 1, Harold Howe, then U.S. commissioner of education, had just read Jeanne Chall's new book, *Learning to Read: The Great Debate.*[6] He stated that it was the first book on reading that had ever made any sense to him and he recommended that John Gardner read it. Secretary Gardner, who had stated, "Some subjects are more important than others. Reading is the most important of all,"[7] read the book and enthusiastically authorized the selection of a Secretary's (HEW) National Advisory Committee on Dyslexia and Related Reading Disorders. The committee of 20 did not begin meeting until August 1968 and submitted its report a year later in August 1969.

The report was a very comprehensive summary of how reading problems are defined and how they are ameliorated, with specific recommendations for a national program having three major components:[8]

1. An Office on Reading Disorders within HEW whose responsibility would be the coordination of a national effort in reading research and development.

2. A network of Operational Reading Research and Development Centers whose responsibilities would be the development of specific procedures and programs for the identification and remediation of children with reading disorders and the analysis of the cost/effectiveness of such procedures and programs.

3. The implementation of measures to increase the quality and availability of training, and the availability of reading researchers, reading specialists, and reading teachers.

The committee made several recommendations concerning national programs, a national office, research, model classrooms, and professional training, but a new administration came along with its own ideas about reading.

1969. The Secretary's National Advisory Committee on Dyslexia and Related Reading Disorders submitted its report on August 19,

1969. It received very little publicity within the reading establishment and none from the general press. A new president had taken over with a new secretary of HEW and a new commissioner of education. With no credit given to the previous administration's work in advancing the cause of reading, most of the committee's recommendations were mentioned just 1 week later on August 23, 1969, when the new commissioner of education, James Allen, made his startling "Right to Read" speech and announced that the goal of the USOE for the 1970s was going to be to solve the reading problem in the United States. It was to be "Education's Moonshot." This was such a popular and generally accepted goal that 6 months later, in his message on education reform, President Nixon stated that the aim of the "Right to Read" program would be to ensure that by 1980 no American would leave school who was not reading up to his capacity.

Nixon appointed his wife, Pat, honorary chairperson of the National Reading Council, a 50-member group that included Al Capp and Glen Campbell.

After Commissioner Allen said that solving the reading problem was a national priority, President Nixon proclaimed the 1970s the "Right to Read Decade." Although he later fired Allen for not having the appropriate political views, Nixon persuaded the USOE to fund a national "Right to Read" effort with discretionary funds, which was money pirated from other federal programs. Plagued by mismanagement, low priority, and not enough money, "Right to Read" did not put any dent in the illiteracy rate right away. It was an example of using the problem to fight the problem—enlisting the aid of The Great American Reading Machine to solve the reading crisis in America.

1970–1975. The first "Right to Read" effort was the establishment of the National Reading Center. In an article in the *Phi Delta Kappan,* in 1972, Congresswoman Edith Green summarized the activities of the ill-fated center.[9]

> The goal of the National Reading Center was to end the nation's illiteracy problem. Who can argue with a goal in which an estimated 18.5 million adults unable to read English should not receive some kind of help?
>
> But the center, which was established in August, 1970, by three members of a White House advisory council on reading, set about accomplishing its objective in a bizarre way. The center's goal was to establish a corps of volunteer tutors, 10 million by 1976 (our two-hundredth anniversary), each volunteer capable and willing to coach an illiterate. From my experience in Washington, the best-known federal "volunteer" pro-

grams are those in which we pay the volunteers, whether it is Volunteers in Service to America, or Peace Corps volunteers, or Teacher Corps volunteers. At the hearings, the secretary of HEW testified that no effort was made to cost out the so-called Ten Million Tutors plan before the USOE gave the center its first grant of $1.5 million. Making the modest assumption that you would have to pay at least half the volunteers and hire reading specialists, my staff members have costed out the scheme at $12.5 billion — nearly three times the entire budget of the Office of Education.

The notion of calling for 10 million volunteers by 1976 to teach reading was bound to fail. After nearly two years and $3 million of the USOE's money, the center has produced a stack of press releases and reports 18 inches high, two national surveys on the extent of illiteracy (a third survey is on its way), 1,000 people who are supposed to train a corps of volunteer reading tutors, and 1.5 million milk cartons with messages thereon exhorting parents to read to their children.

About nine months after the USOE gave the center its first-year grant, a USOE audit alleged that the center had misspent $305,300, largely in public relations and architectural fees for impressive Washington office surroundings at 1776 Masschusetts Avenue, N.W. Some estimate the historical "1776" address cost many thousands beyond this figure. With all these problems, the USOE is planning to fund this non-profit organization for a third year.

In June 1973, the National Reading Center was terminated. After its failure, the federal "Right to Read" program slowly began to make headway, especially under Ruth Holloway as director. The program has directly funded school and community reading programs and has underwritten 31 state education agencies for state reading programs. In 1974 it funded 33 teacher education institutions to develop innovative reading teacher education programs. In 1975 Ruth Holloway resigned her position to become superintendent of the Oakland, California, school system and a temporary director was assigned.

The "Right to Read" effort continues to be the federal government's only direct attack on illiteracy. However, it has one fatal flaw. It is designed to filter money through established institutions—The Great American Reading Machine. Because the problems of illiteracy are so complex and so national—that is, spread across schools in every community in every state in the country—the federal government has simplified solutions to their lowest common denominators. I'm sure this is a politically wise thing to do. But like most federal programs, if one attempts to please all the people all the time, the people will raise hell when funding stops. Title I of the 1964 ESEA is a program that has spent millions of dollars in virtually every community in the country. The Title I program has been the largest single program of the USOE since 1964 in terms of dollars spent. While other poverty programs have been killed or decreased by Congress, Title I continues to be funded at a high rate. Why? Because the program affects constituents in practically every congressman's district. I have heard of no Title I program that has made any great impact or supplied any innovations, yet Title I monies are so institutionalized that they are expected each year as part of the regular operating budgets in most school systems. "Right to Read" programs appear to be heading in the same direction—diluted across the country to such an extent that the total impact is negligible. But, because the programs are so widespread, to vote to cut them off is politically unwise for congressional representatives—so they persist, good or bad.

From 1974 to 1976, President Ford vetoed almost every new education bill and continued to cut the programs begun by the Johnson administration. Despite Ford's antieducation stand, in 1975 Congress passed a National Reading Improvement Act, which promised even more possible money to fight reading problems. Although very little was authorized to fund the act in 1977 and 1978, it may also fail for the same reason—filtering money through an institution that has a record of failure. The Carter administration hopefully will put some imagination into federal reading education programs.

The major question is, How can federal money be utilized to the best advantage? We need a wholly different approach. If not, history is bound to repeat itself, even with people with the best of intentions. Perhaps the Children's Television Workshop has one successful model—that is, steering clear of educators for the purpose of producing television shows that worked. I believe that is *why* it worked. But we need trained reading teachers to teach children to read. Given the present oversupply of teachers, now is the time to attract bright, enthusiastic, dedicated individuals into our teacher education institutions and allow them to pursue programs leading toward a classroom reading specialist degree. Under federal funding, such programs would produce new personnel and allow local schools to renew their teaching staffs with a new kind of teacher. The kind of training program I would recommend is described in Chap. 11.

Congress and the general public are periodically made aware of the misuse of federal funds, but I think the general public is unaware of how funds are awarded, as indicated by my taxpaying neighbor. When I told him about how I consulted for the federal government, his reaction was, "Oh, I'm paying your salary these days, eh? Another one of those government grants." Sometimes individuals or cities get government funds because of the influence of a powerful congressman or senator. Usually they are awarded on the basis of competitive proposals. Of course, some funds are awarded directly to each of the 50 states, and others are awarded to schools based on the number of pupils or on the number of educationally disadvantaged pupils in a district. But many programs require colleges, universities, public schools, or other eligible education agencies to write proposals for how they would spend the money were they awarded a grant. The government advertises the availability of the funds through a magazine called the *Federal Register* and sets a deadline date after which they will not accept proposals. The government also provides detailed guidelines or proposal outlines specifying what must be in the proposal. So the education agency, your child's school for example, must read the *Federal Register* to know whether funds are available for particular programs. Once school officials know about the program, they must request copies of the proposal guidelines. Then they must plan a program which promises to be successful and write a proposal for its funding. Most colleges, universities, and successful school systems have been hiring a person—usually called a federal projects coordinator—whose full-time job is to be aware of new programs and write proposals for funding. Once proposals are sent to Washington, it usually takes several months until decisions are made as to which proposals are funded. In most cases USOE asks professionals from outside of Washington to read and evaluate proposals. I did so for USOE for a period of 3 years. For one research project, ten proposals were funded out of 150 received. Competition is fierce, but the competitors are not necessarily the schools with the greatest need. The schools with the greatest need are usually the least knowledgable about how to compete for federal dollars.

State and Local Governments

The increased financial involvement of the federal government has served to increase the involvement of state and local agencies because the money filters down to them.

After graduation from college, the teacher's first professional contact is usually with a state education department, for it is through this department that the teacher becomes legally certified to teach.

Each state education department has an official who monitors the reading and language arts programs in the state. There is even a national organization of such people, the Association of State English and Reading Supervisors (ASEARS). Although different states have different job descriptions, the person who heads this department on the state level usually has some authority over money allocations and state programs. The reading experts in the state are usually friendly with this supervisor. He or she often teaches an extension course for the state university at the state capital. Allocations for federal Title I and Title III programs—of ESEA—are often made by this person to his or her friends. There are now "Right to Read" coordinators in 31 of the 50 states. In many states this coordinator is the same person as the reading coordinator mentioned above.

At the local level, it is more a matter of how money is used to manipulate than where it comes from. Local administrators—the superintendent, his or her assistants, the principals, and reading administrators—usually owe allegiance to the local or state college or university from which they graduated. Often, college professors more readily grant a master's or doctoral degree to a local school administrator who plays the game, that is, is willing to negotiate such things as:

- money for a research study
- in-service training programs run by the college
- student teaching sites
- future jobs in the school system

Governments, at every level, play a significant role in the operation of The Great American Reading Machine. They provide the largest financial influence, but not the only influence.

References

1. Green, Edith, "Education's Federal Grab Bag," *Phi Delta Kappan*, October 1972, vol. 54, pp. 84–85.
2. Penney, Monte, and Hjelm, Howard, "The Targeted Research and Development Program on Reading," *American Educational Research Journal*, vol. 7, No. 3, May 1970, p. 426.
3. "It is likely that improvement in reading instruction can be brought about more efficiently by improved selection and training of teachers, by improved in-service training programs, and by improved school learning climates than by instituting changes in instructional materials," From Dykstra, Robert, "Classroom Implications of the First-Grade Studies," in *Professional Focus on Reading* (Proceedings of the CRA conference), edited by Clay Ketcham, vol. 9, 1968, pp. 53–59.
4. Penney, Monte, and Hjelm, Howard, *loc. cit.*
5. Penney, Monte, and Hjelm, Howard, *op. cit.*, p. 429.

6. Chall, Jeanne, *Learning to Read: The Great Debate,* McGraw-Hill Book Co., New York, 1967.

7. Gardner, John W., "National Goals in Education," in *Goals for Americans,* Prentice-Hall, Inc., Englewood Cliffs, N.J., 1960, p. 86.

8. HEW National Advisory Committee on Dyslexia and Related Reading Disorders, *"Reading Disorders in the United States,"* Developmental Learning Materials, Chicago, August 1969, pp. 26–28.

9. Green, Edith, *op. cit.,* p. 85.

FOUR

PUBLISHING

William Holmes McGuffey, the first author to publish a set of graded basal readers, can be said to be the father of the American basal reader. He made a grand total of $1,000 in his contract with Truman and Smith of Cincinnati. His readers have sold over 122 million copies over the years since 1836. His nineteenth-century readers were graded by difficulty—the 3rd reader was more difficult than the 2nd and so on. By today's "grade-level" criteria, McGuffey's 3rd reader would be about 7th-grade level. It wasn't long after the McGuffey readers appeared that more and more publishers were producing sets of "basal" readers which were "graded"—that is, the 3rd reader was written at a 3rd-grade reading level and was meant to be used in the 3rd grade, the 4th reader for the 4th grade, and so on. These graded basal readers were to become the hallmark of the elementary school—one book for each child, a set of basal readers in every classroom.

More money can be made by publishing a set of basal readers than in any other area of publishing. "Just think, 12 classrooms in an average elementary school. Thirty kids in every room. That's 360 books multiplied by all the schools in the city, multiplied by all the cities in the state." This statement by a typical publisher's representative is correct. In the above example, one typical city of 200,000 people would have about 55 schools and spend about $160,000 on basal readers. If an author makes, say, 5 percent of the net sales and the sales are $80,000 in one city, then from one city's sales the author makes $4,000. Multiply that times 100 cities . . . and so on.

Another indication of the profits to be made in school publishing is the number of large corporations that have purchased publishing firms. When one realizes that every child in the country in public elementary schools (30.4 million, in 1975; USOE projects 33 million in 1978[1]) probably has a reading book that costs around $10 per book (the average cost in 1978), it is easy to see that there are millions of dollars to be made. The USOE reported that in 1972 more than 45 billion dollars

35

was spent on elementary and secondary schools in the country, and even if less than 2 percent went for teaching materials, that's still almost 1 billion dollars. Publishers have long been attacked for the dull subject matter of Dick, Jane, Alice, and Jerry, and more recently on sexist and racist grounds. They are beginning to respond with newer editions which, of course, mean more and more profits.

The reading business includes more than just basal readers. For elementary and secondary classes there are workbooks, games, trade books (stories other than graded basals), paperbacks, drill cards, boxes, kits, films, and filmstrips. The college-textbook trade includes all the books about *teaching* reading. A college professor of reading hasn't really made it in the publish-or-perish world until he has published his book on how to teach reading. Neither the professor nor the publisher gets rich on these books, but they persist. The table of contents of a typical textbook on the teaching of reading reveals the same boring, noncontroversial subject matter of such books of 5, 10, 15, and 20 years ago. The same old stuff in a new wrapper—

- Readiness for Reading
- Teaching Beginning Reading
- Word-Analysis Skills
- Teaching Comprehension
- Materials for Teaching Reading
- Recommended Practices through the Grades
- Remedial Reading
- New Ideas and the Future

—or some slight variation thereof. The last chapter is usually the shortest. These books are usually written by a professor who has become a well-known reading specialist, either through publication of another book on reading, through elected office in the International Reading Association, or through the nurturing of one of his or her former professors, who is already an established figure in the area.

Textbooks used in reading-teacher education courses abound. There are at least 30 on the market now and at least half of those are revisions of books originally published 20 years ago. If you've read one, you've read them all. A review by George Weber of two textbooks published in 1969 indicates the general quality of most reading texts. In criticizing these two texts, Weber stated:

> In the first place, they are poorly written. I will spare the reader a lengthy list of the examples that could be cited. It should suffice to say that they are not any better than most textbooks used in education courses. They are replete with pomposity, vagueness, platitudes, and irrelevant material.

Worst of all, they are poorly organized and conceptually very confused.

Secondly, the books are outdated in many respects. The overstuffed bibliographies must have been compiled for the most part some years ago. But of more significance, there is no mention of several important recent studies in the field.

Finally, these books fundamentally support the discredited whole-word, look-say approach to reading instruction, although the author now decries the extremely limited vocabulary and vapid content of its basal readers. This support is hardly surprising, since [the author] was himself a co-author of a basal-reader series which uses that approach, and he has long been associated with it.[2]

If an author is unsuccessful in finding a reputable publisher for his book, he can always turn to one of the many so-called "vanity presses." A vanity publisher will publish a book, no matter what its quality, if the author is a college professor and can guarantee enough sales so that the vanity publisher can make a profit. To fulfill this requirement, a professor need only require that his book be purchased by all of his students. So professors get their biases in front of students one way or another. How many college courses have you taken from the Professor Schmaltzes only to discover that the required text for the course is "How to _____," by (guess who?) Professor Schmaltz?

When I was director of the reading program at the University of Massachusetts School of Education (1968–1972), the School of Education was gaining a reputation as the most innovative in the country. As the word spread, publishers' representatives began to visit the school more and more frequently. In the fall of 1970, I was often called upon by publishers' representatives. Most started out rather indirectly. "Are you doing any writing yourself?" Even though I had never published a book, my association with an innovative school of education led several publishers to invite me to write a reading textbook for them—whether I had proven I knew anything about reading or not. They were begging for a reading textbook that would have some "pizzazz."

Jeanne Chall commented on the influence publishers have on schools and school systems:

> In my visits to schools I found evidence over and over again that the companies that publish beginning reading materials play an important role in determining how children are taught to read. The representatives (salesmen) of these companies are very able and persuasive, and many school administrators listen to them carefully. One administrator told me, "The publishers' representatives are often more informed than the

principals and teachers, who don't have the time to be informed." Another specifically noted that it was the representative of a publisher, calling with a new program, who convinced the people in his school what reading program to adopt.

Once they have sold a set of materials to a school system, the publishers continue to influence the teaching of reading in that system. We have seen how important the teaching manuals that accompany the reading materials are to most teachers. In addition, the publishers distribute newsletters, promotional materials, and reprints of articles by authorities. They also contribute significantly to in-service and teacher education through demonstration and training programs.

This behavior on the part of publishers' representatives may seem petty and childish, but there is, in fact, a good reason for it. Producing a reading series involves a very large financial commitment on the part of the publisher. The decision of a single school system, especially a large one, to adopt a given set of materials automatically ensures a large number of sales. Further, the sale of materials, even on a small scale, is often used by the publishing house as evidence that a school system has given these materials its approval. If it is a particularly large school system, this information carries a great deal of weight. Convincing school systems to adopt a new program is a difficult job, requiring all the persuasion a publisher's representative can come up with. Large school systems, especially, develop various criteria for the selection of teaching materials that become a fixed part of general policy, even though they may be based on questionable research evidence and may, in fact, be wrong. Often this policy may keep a school system from trying out something new unless it is presented with the most convincing arguments for doing so.[3]

In addition to keeping mediocrity alive in method and technique in teaching reading and inhibiting change, the publishers' basal readers perpetuate two other concepts that have become so entrenched in our thinking that they have not been questioned. They are the notions that there are *grade levels* of children's reading ability and there are *readability levels* of books.

Grade Levels

Have you ever heard of a child who isn't *mathing* up to grade level, or who isn't *social studying* up to grade level, or who isn't *sciencing* up to grade level? But your child is expected to be *reading* up to grade level. A child's reading grade level is determined by the highest level book the child can read while making a minimum of word-recognition or word-analysis errors. If a child can read a book written at the 3rd-grade level with 95 percent accuracy (that is, pronouncing no fewer than 95 words correctly in a 100-word sample) and reads a 4th-grade-level book with only 70 percent accuracy, it is said that the child is reading on the 3rd-grade level. If a child with normal intelligence is not reading "up to grade level" (that is, the child's reading grade level is lower than the grade the child is assigned to in school) or if the child's reading grade level is lower than the grade level one would expect based on an intelligence test score, the child is said to have a reading problem. These are the criteria used by every school, every classroom teacher, and every reading teacher in the country. They either compare the child's "reading level" to the grade the child is in (the less desirable criterion) or the grade one would expect the child to function at based on the child's ability (the more desirable criterion). Both criteria are faulty because of the use of "reading levels."

The concept of reading levels probably goes back to 1836, when McGuffey first published his famous readers. At that time, *McGuffey's Eclectic Readers* were labeled primer, 1st, 2nd, and on through 6th. The intention then, in the one-room schools, was for the child to begin the 3rd reader after finishing the 2nd reader and so on, regardless of what "grade" the child was in.

I collect old McGuffey readers. Several years ago I bought a box of books at a country auction in Ohio and in the bottom of the box was the teacher's daily register from an old one-room country school. The register, part of which is reproduced on the following page, is an attendance log book and a record of the achievement of the children. This particular book covered the years from 1855 to 1866. I was not surprised at the wide range of achievement or the wide range of readers being read by children of the same age. In many classrooms today, children are reading books of varying difficulty, but it is very alarming to visit and hear of classrooms where *every single student in the 4th grade is reading the 4th reader!*

In many of today's elementary school classrooms, children in the 4th grade *are* reading from the 4th-grade reader, regardless of ability. Each reader today is written specifically for one grade level. If a child finishes the 2nd-grade book halfway through the 2nd-grade year and wants to go to the 3rd reader, the teacher or the principal will ask, "What will the 3rd-grade teacher use if I let the child have a 3rd-grade book now?" The answer, of course, should be, "Who cares, so long as the child is reading and progressing?" Eventually, the 3rd- or 4th-grade teacher gets children who are bored by reading because they have not been challenged. The solution to the problem, of course, was

13

Grades of reading

3reader		Age
Ellen Rose	4	8
Noah Wilson	4	14
Emkney Day	4	11
Polly L Campbell	5	8
George do	5	14
Alexander Rose	8	11
Ruben Wood	4	10
John Wcomb	5	12

4 Reader		
Jenkin Jones	4	14
Rebacca Wright	2	10
Evaline Rose	8	12
David Jones	8	15
Mary J pros	8	15
Sarah M Wright	8	15
Orlsina Rose	4	15
William Wood	2	12

5 Reader		
James Calen	8	19

invented by McGuffey, not his content but his concept of making each reader more difficult than the previous one without "grade levels." Teachers who allow children to progress through the readers as quickly as they individually can are, unfortunately, few in number. If the children are bored, good teachers let them read something that turns them on.

Readability Levels

Closely related to the notion that there are grade levels of children's reading ability is the notion that there are readability levels of books. Both are an attempt to quantify something which is not quantifiable.

What is a readability level? Beginning about the middle of the nineteenth century, when graded reading books really caught on in schools and publishers were competing madly for sales, one reading book was simply a little more difficult than the previous one in terms of sentence length, number of syllables in words, and length of story.

> The grading of books by age was at first, however, nonexistent; the lessons were merely graded within each book. Grading among books began to appear near midcentury, but without any uniformity among publishers, and without any external standards. Thus a third Reader in one series may bear little relationship in degree of difficulty to a third Reader in another series, nor may either have anything to do with the third grade in school. In each case the third Reader may simply be the third in point of difficulty in that particular series of Readers. Near the end of the century professional educators took an increasing interest in such matters, and grading became more uniform. By this time too the hand of the professional educator can be clearly discerned in the simplification of vocabulary and the introduction of pedagogical aids of all sorts.[4]

By the 1920s and 1930s, readability formulas began to appear, which predicted the "readability level" of a book. To determine readability formulas, 20,000 words were classified according to their frequency of occurrence or the number of syllables per word, and words per sentence were counted in a 100-word sample of the material. Then, by applying a complicated formula, a readability level was assigned to a book.

The unfortunate point, and reading educators have known it for years but have done nothing about it, is that one cannot assign a readability or grade level to a word or an idea. At what grade level would you assign such one-syllable words as sin, death, sex, war, hate, love, kill, and four-letter obscenities? Although all these words are short, one-syllable words, they do not appear in primers or 1st-grade readers, and rightfully so.

Readability formulas have been applied to basal readers as well as to all the other trade books that are used in elementary schools. As a matter of fact, many elementary libraries are catalogued and ordered by readability levels. Book companies advertise their wares by readability level, not by literary value or interest. Following is an excerpt from a book catalog.

Readability Level Catalog

This listing of carefully selected library books now includes a unique feature never before available from any other source. For the first time in publishing history, the actual readability levels of thousands of books offered by Follett Library Book Company are noted. Thus, in addition to all the information usually given to aid in careful purchasing of library and supplementary books, this catalog also indicates the exact reading level for which each book is most suitable.

The teachers and librarians who spent months analyzing the vocabulary and sentence lengths in these thousands of books are proud to make this contribution to the art of book selection. They are also rewarded in knowing that through the courtesy of the Follett Library Book Company, this significant effort will be available to all other educators who are concerned with bringing the world of literature to children.[5]

It is important to note how these books are classified. One would think that authors of basal readers and trade books would pick out classics in children's literature that would be appropriate for schools, apply readability tests to the books, and arrive at a readability level. That might have been how it was 30 years ago, but not today. Authors and publishers respond to the consumers' (teachers) demands for graded books. The author of the graded-reader series writes with the readability formula in hand. In writing a 3rd reader, for example, he cannot use words longer than two syllables or sentences longer than seven words. This accounts for the bland, often stilted content of most school readers.

The authors of standarized tests then use the same material to evaluate reading ability. If a child makes a certain number of mistakes in a book written for a certain grade level, it is easily determined that he is reading at or below that grade level.

Estimating the readability levels of books in various disciplines has become a favorite pastime of authors, editors, and publishers, resulting in the fact that practically every book in a typical elementary school library has a grade level assigned to it. Although readability formulas have always been merely *predictors* of readability levels, once the formulas have been applied, reading teachers have adopted them as precise and inviolate.

Lists of frequently used words and the syllable count and sentence-length count are the most popular methods of assigning readability levels. Other methods of predicting readability have been suggested, such as:

1. Using the cloze procedure, deleting a word every so often, or deleting words randomly, and then checking to see how difficult the passage is to comprehend with the words missing.
2. Using syntactic complexity, that is, word arrangements or sentence structures, to determine difficulty.

But the fact remains that readability formulas and reading levels are false means of quantifying reading or of labeling children in order to evaluate their relative abilities. Assigning grade levels to books and children turns out to be an insidious form of censorship and indoctrination.

The authors of the graded readers, reading materials, and textbooks on teaching reading are frequently the same people. Most successful authors have published both a reading series and a textbook for teachers. The majority are college or university professors who studied with a successful author of an earlier work. Huge economic rewards have created a system in which successful professors are asked either to write or to lend his or her name to a set of basal readers. When one thinks of authors in the reading business, the list of names on page 44 comes to mind immediately. A complete listing would take five pages or more.

Students and colleagues of these authors have since taken over the lucrative business of writing reading books. In some cases, Scott Foresman for example, the series is so popular that a team of authors has been named so that 10 or more authors share the profits of authorship of one of the best-selling major basal-reader series.

In addition to furthering the notions of grade levels and readability levels, the authors and publishers continue the myth that reading is the only way to learn. Reading is placed on a pedestal. Reading teachers claim that reading is the only essential skill that a child must learn, excluding all other media for communication. Lacking the ability to read, a child cannot be successful in school. A non-

Name	University	Basal Reader	Date
1. William S. Gray[6]	University of Chicago	*The Curriculum Foundation Series,* the Scott, Foresman readers (These are the first Dick and Jane readers)	1927
2. Nila Banton Smith[7]	New York University	*Learning to Read,* Silver Burdett readers	1940
3. Paul Witty[8]	Northwestern University	*Reading for Interest,* D.C. Heath readers	1946
4. Emmett Betts[9]	Temple University	*Betts Basic Readers*	1948
5. David Russell[9]	University of Saskatchewan	*Ginn Basic Readers*	1948
6. Paul McKee[11]	Michigan State University	*Reading for Meaning,* Houghton, Mifflin readers	1950
7. Guy Bond[12]	University of Minnesota	*The Developmental Reading Series*	1950
8. William Sheldon[13]	Syracuse University	*Sheldon Basic Readers,* Allyn and Bacon	1957
9. Russell Stauffer[14]	University of Delaware	*The Winston Basic Readers*	1960
10. Albert Harris[15]	Queens College	*The Macmillan Reading Program*	1965

reader, young or old, is handicapped in trying to get along in the world. In a letter from the Book-of-the-Month Club, Inc., advertising a "reading skills program, a home training program for students of high school and college age," sponsored by Rutgers University in 1963, a self-administered test, purported to:

> PINPOINT whatever faulty reading habits the youngster may already have acquired, this may be the beginning of FAR EASIER LEARNING *through all the rest of his educational career.*

It may actually decide whether or not he can get into a college of his choice, and how well he does there. Indeed, it may well turn out to be of critical importance in ultimately determining whether or not he succeeds in whatever he later undertakes as an adult.[16]

In countless other publications, the American public is led to believe that if a child can't read well, the child will be an intellectual cripple, an unsuccessful person, a failure in life, denied opportunities, handicapped for life, etc. Reading professionals want the public to believe that what they have to offer is the key to success in life.

Unfortunately, reading *is* the key to success for the very people who fail at reading more than any others—blacks and other minority groups. If a white, middle-class child fails at reading, he can rely on the color television, trips with his family, and all the other opportunities for learning many times denied to minorities. Black and other minority children, who need to learn to read for *survival,* must learn in book-oriented schools.

Newspapers, Magazines, and Journals

Most articles on reading that appear in the popular newspapers and magazines are written by reading professionals. Although often written for the layman rather than the professional, the attitudes or values espoused are usually those of professionals. The journals are the prime offenders. It is through this medium that the college and university "publish-or-perish" syndrome is vented. Because colleges use the publication of articles as evidence of competence for professors, unnecessary educational journals and reading journals prosper. Most educational journals are the voice of one of the hundreds of professional educational organizations. Some are simply slick commercial ventures.

The largest professional reading organization, the International Reading Association (IRA) (membership 65,000 plus), publishes three journals: *The Reading Teacher, Journal of Reading,* and *Reading Research Quarterly. (The Reading Teacher* and *Journal of Reading* have a combined circulation of over 68,000.) Each journal has an editorial advisory board made up of 15 or so "reading experts" whose job it is to read manuscripts submitted to the journal for publication. Members of the editorial advisory board read the articles "blind," that is, with no knowledge of the author's name or title. At least two editorial advisory board members read each article. This procedure attempts to negate any possible bias on the part of the editor in choosing articles for publication. In the 1974–1975 school year, 682 manuscripts were submitted to *The Reading Teacher* and the *Journal of Reading.* The editor reported that more than half of the contributors identified themselves as working in a college or university. During the year more than 75 percent of the manuscripts received were rejected. In the 1973–1974 school year, the rejection rate was 75 percent for *The Reading Teacher* and 66 percent for *Journal of Reading.* Most college and university professors of reading submit articles to the IRA before they try the state reading journal or the journals of lesser organizations. There are at least 30 of these less prestigious journals published by state reading-teacher organizations in half of the 50 states and by regional reading organizations. Judging from the quality of the articles as I view them, it appears that the journals serve the publish-or-perish rule rather than contribute ideas to promote better teaching of reading.

Besides the journals of the reading organizations and professional organizations such as Phi Delta Kappa, a national educational honor fraternity which publishes the *Phi Delta Kappan,* articles about reading often appear in *Saturday Review, Psychology Today, McCall's,* and other popular magazines. In these magazines one is likely to find articles on "teaching your baby to read," "patterning for language learning," and "speed reading made easy." Such articles offer the lay reader a little bit of biased knowledge about reading, which results in making the reading teacher's job more difficult when parents ask questions based on them.

Every few years publishers and pitchmen introduce new speed-reading programs. Speed-reading courses have profited since the widely advertised fact that President Kennedy had taken such a course. In 1973, the American Express Company advertised a program by asking "What's better than speed reading?—Speed learning, speed plus comprehension." For only $110, one could purchase a set of books and cassette recordings which would provide a "combined speed-reading–thinking–comprehension–remembering–learning program," according to the promotional brochure. The program was developed by a reading professor ("one of the country's leading reading experts"). I think the speed-reading merchants promise more than they can deliver, but the delivery system is so neat that once hooked the student can never admit he's been had. Speed-reading courses cost from $150 to $300 per course. When someone has paid such a high fee, he would never admit that he didn't get anything out of the course. This psychological gimmick, along with the promise of greater comprehension for college students and the prestige of speed-reading politicians, has served to perpetuate speed-reading courses. They are offered for credit in high schools, colleges, and adult-education programs and for profit in large cities all over the country.

Several researchers have studied graduates of speed-reading courses and have found that they read no faster than it is physically possible to read, that is, 600 to 900 words per minute.[17–19] However, the speed-reading merchants do not define reading as seeing every word. They teach a fast, skimming technique. It gets to be a little ridiculous when promises are made in advertisements that you can learn to read a book faster than it is physically possible to turn the pages.

Most adults in our country, including college graduates, read at a very slow rate—around 250 words per minute. It is possible, with easy material, to triple this rate to 750 words per minute and still call it reading. A good reader adjusts his or her reading rate to the difficulty of the material and to his or her purpose for reading. Most of us tend to read everything at the same rate. In the words of Walter Pauk, well-known reading professor at Cornell University, "Most students read the back of the cereal box at the breakfast table with the same rapt attention that they read their physics textbooks."

We know that there is a direct relationship between speed of reading and comprehension, that is, understanding what one has read. There are at least two levels of comprehension. One is literal comprehension or remembering what the author stated. "What color was the girl's dress?" and "How many boys were in the group?" are literal comprehension questions. The other, and more difficult level is interpretation—being able to answer such questions as, "What did the author mean?" "Why did such and such happen?" "What caused the man to act that way?" Therefore, a mature reader is a flexible reader, one who can adjust rate of reading to the difficulty of the material and to purpose. The speed-reading merchants lead students and businessmen to believe that they can complete their reading in a shorter time with more comprehension. A more appropriate approach would be to slow them down on difficult material to guarantee better comprehension. Students and businessmen do not read "easy" material. The speed-reading racket is so pervasive in high schools, colleges, and businesses that speed-reading is often the only contact the general public has with the reading field. For that reason, I have devoted a chapter to the speed-reading merchants (Chap. 9).

The major concern of publishers and pitchmen is profits, and they are readily available in the reading business. Teacher education has a different goal.

References

1. U.S. Department of HEW, Office of Education, "Statistics of Public Elementary and Secondary Day Schools," Fall 1972.
2. Weber, George, "ACBE Review of Texts for Reading at Graduate and Undergraduate Levels," *Phi Delta Kappan*, vol. 50, June 1969, p. 609.
3. Chall, Jeanne, *Learning to Read: The Great Debate*, McGraw-Hill Book Co., New York, 1967, pp. 297–299.
4. Elson, Ruth, *Guardians of Tradition, American Schoolbooks of the Nineteenth Century*, University of Nebraska Press, Lincoln, 1964, p. 5.
5. *1971–1972 Catalog*, Follett Library Book Co., Chicago, 1971.
6. Gray, William, et al., *The Curriculum Foundation Program*, Scott, Foresman & Co., Chicago, 1927, revised 1965.
7. Smith, Nila B., *Learning to Read*, Silver Burdett and Co., New York, 1940–1945.
8. Witty, Paul A., *Reading for Interest*, D.C. Heath and Co., Boston, 1942. revised 1946, 1955.
9. Betts, Emmett A., and Welch, Carolyn M., *Betts Basic Readers*, American Book Co., New York, 1948–1951, revised 1964.
10. Russell, David, et al., *The Ginn Basic Readers*, Ginn & Co., Boston, 1948–1951, revised 1964.
11. McKee, Paul, et al., *Reading for Meaning*, Houghton, Mifflin Co., Boston, 1950, revised 1957, 1963.
12. Bond, Guy L., et al., *The Developmental Reading Series*, Lyons and Carnahan, Chicago, 1950–58, revised 1962.
13. Sheldon, William D., et al., *Sheldon Basic Readers*, Allyn and Bacon, Inc., Boston, 1957.
14. Stauffer, Russell G., Burrows, Alvina, T., et al., *The Winston Basic Readers*, Communication Program, John C. Winston Co., Philadelphia, 1960–1962.
15. Harris, Albert J., Clark, Mae Knight, et al., *The Macmillan Reading Program*, Macmillan Co., New York, 1965.
16. Reading Skills, *A Training Program for Students*, Sponsored by Rutgers University, Book-of-The-Month Club, Inc., Direct-Mail Advertisement, 1963.
17. Spache, George D., "Is This a Breakthrough in Reading?" *The Reading Teacher*, vol. 15, January 1962, pp. 258–263.
18. Taylor, Stanford, E., *Eye Movements and Reading: Facts and Fallacies*, Educational Developmental Laboratories, Huntington, N.Y., November 1963.
19. Taylor, Stanford, E., "An Evaluation of Forty-one Trainees Who Had Recently Completed the 'Reading Dynamics' Program," in *Eleventh Yearbook of the National Reading Conference*, 1962, pp. 41–56.

FIVE

TEACHER EDUCATION

Nowhere in education are poor teaching techniques used as much as in "reading methods" courses. These are the courses recommended by the International Reading Association (IRA) and the State Department of Education Teacher Certification Boards: the courses which one *must* take if one is to become a teacher.

In 1961, the Carnegie Foundation sponsored a study of teacher education in reading. Mary Austin and Coleman Morrison,[1] then at Harvard University, reported on interview and questionnaire data collected from colleges and universities which prepared reading teachers. They found reading-teacher education to be in a state of confused, incompetent mediocrity. Their 22 recommendations generally would have improved reading-teacher education had they been followed. More than 15 years later, however, such criticisms as poor selection of reading materials for students, poor liberal arts backgrounds of teacher trainees, dull education professors, few alternatives, and rigid lecture-format courses are still valid. Some of their key recommendations were as follows:

Recommendation 2:

That students be permitted (if not encouraged) to elect a field of concentration other than elementary education, provided basic requirements in the education program are met, including the equivalent of a three semester hour course in the teaching of reading, and one course in student teaching.

Recommendation 4:

That senior faculty members, prominent in the field of reading, play a more active role in the instruction of undergraduates and assume responsibility for teaching at least one undergraduate course.

Recommendation 7:

That college instructors continue to emphasize that no one method of word recognition, such as phonetic analysis, be

49

PREFACE.

HAVING been an examiner for many years, the author has watched, with the deepest interest, the results developed in the examination of hundreds, nay thousands, of candidates for the Teacher's profession. While some of them have been gratifying, most have been sufficiently surprising and painful.

The facts are these:

1st. A considerable number of those applying, from year to year, are rejected, because they *totally fail* to sustain the requisite examination.

2d. A larger number *barely* pass the ordeal, and receive certificates scarcely less discreditable than would be rejection itself.

3d. Quite 25 per cent. of the remainder pass the required examination about half as well as they ought, and receive certificates accordingly.

4th. Not more than 10 per cent., hardly more than 5 per cent. of the whole, secure the highest testimonials of scholarship which the law puts fairly within the reach of all.

Why is this? A few, doubtless, are *mentally* disqualified; and the business of teaching is the last in which they should have thought of engaging. But the great mass of candidates remains, and the question still urges itself, Why should so many of these continue to disgrace themselves, and disappoint their friends, by failure to sustain a reputable examination? Why should the great majority of them continue to subject themselves to the trouble and expense of a re-examination every 4, 6, 9, or 12 months, when they might have exemption from all this for a much longer period?

Convinced that there is no necessity for this state of things, and that he who shall point out a reasonable method of avoiding it will be doing an acceptable service, the author has prepared this work, earnestly hoping that it will contribute, in some degree, at least, to a higher and more thorough grade of qualification on the part of candidates for the important and responsible position of the Teacher.

(iii)

From *The Examiner or Teacher's Aid,* designed to assist pupils in reviewing their studies, teachers in examining their classes, and normal schools and teachers institutes in class and drill exercises. By Alexander Duncan and A.M. Wilson, Hinkle and Co., Cincinnati, 1863.

used to the exclusion of other word attack techniques, and that students be exposed to a variety of opinions related to other significant issues of reading, such as grouping policies, pre-reading materials, techniques of beginning reading instruction, and teaching machines.

Recommendation 9:

That a course in basic reading instruction be required of *all* prospective secondary school teachers.

Recommendation 21:

That colleges re-examine the criteria used to evaluate students during the practice teaching experience to ensure that a passing grade in practice teaching does in fact mean that the student has achieved the desired level of competency in teaching reading and other elementary grade skills.*

Austin and Morrison were not the only ones to call for change during the 1960s. Admiral Hyman Rickover commented on teacher education:

. . . Nor will people whose I.Q. is high enough to be in the "professional range" submit to certification requirements demanding attendance at the kind of dreary "education" courses we inflict on our teachers. That we look upon public school teachers as technicians rather than professionals is revealed by excessive emphasis on pedagogy and neglect of subject matter in American Teacher training programs and certification requirements. Educational officialdom, self-dominated as it is by school administrators and "teachers of the teachers," has the curious idea that what makes a teacher a "professional" is his having taken a specified number of courses in pedagogy. And, what is odder still, that courses in school administration make a person not only a "professional" educator but one of higher rank than the teacher.[2]

In 1970, Wayne Otto and Kenneth Dulin[3] reported a survey they had done among college and university professors of reading who belonged to the National Reading Conference, a national organization of reading specialists. The study was not definitive because of the small sample of professors responding: 67. But they were a sample of reading professors from all over the country. The professors were asked to rank 16 of their professional activities by importance to themselves:

---

*Austin and Morrison, pages 142–156.[1] Austin and Morrison completed a follow-up questionnaire study in 1977 (*The Torch Lighters Revisited,* I R A , Newark, Del., 1977). The follow-up is very supportive of teacher education. But questionnaire data like these are extremely invalid. Who wouldn't say in 1977 that they were following the advice of 1961?

- Among all of the reading professors responding, under-graduate teacher preparation *ranked 11th* among the 16 activities.
- Among "large university" reading professors, undergraduate teacher preparation *ranked 13th* among 16 activities.
- Among "research-oriented" reading professors, under-graduate teacher preparation *ranked 12th* among 16 activities.

The responses of reading professors whose major responsibility was teacher preparation ranked teacher training 13th among 16 activities! The professors valued such things as writing, leadership in organizations, graduate-level teaching, and supervising programs more highly than their primary job—teaching teachers how to teach reading! Colleges and universities reward professors (in dollars) more highly for those other 12 activities. The major criteria for promotion and salary increases at most colleges and universities are teaching, research, and service, but the old publish-or-perish rule really dominates. Naturally, to survive, professors carry out the kinds of activities that are rewarded. Everyone has to teach and there is no way to evaluate it, so they claim. However, not everyone can publish and speak at national meetings, and that's where the pecking order is established. If good teaching is not rewarded, one does what is rewarded or loses a job. The tenure system works in just the opposite way. After a professor has been on a faculty for 6 years or so, has published the required number of research studies, and has not rocked the boat, he is awarded tenure in the job. He cannot be fired. This job security system supposedly protects academic freedom, but in reality it protects many poor teachers from losing their jobs. In a time of recession, depression, and tight money, as it is at this writing, many excellent but nontenured professors are losing their jobs, caught in budget cuts and by the fact that tenured professors can't be fired.

As in any academic area, when students take a course in reading, they get a course in the person teaching it. It is as false to say that every student taking Education 232, "The Teaching of Reading," at X university gets the same course, no matter who teaches it, as it is to say that all 3rd-grade children get 3rd-grade at Y elementary school. They get Mrs. S. or Ms. B. When asked how good a course is or how good an elementary school is, I always respond that a school is as good as the professor teaching the course or the teacher your son or daughter has this year. Human beings have biases, prejudices, and different interests and emphases, and students are sometimes not aware that they may not be hearing all the alternatives or every side of a controversial issue. Jeanne Chall reported the reactions of administrators and teachers to their reading courses as follows:

Those who discussed the effect of their education on their later attitudes commented that what they had learned in their own college courses had worked to prevent them from considering new ideas freely. One school principal . . . attributed his reluctance to investigate the merits of a phonic emphasis to the prejudice that had been instilled in him during his course work at the local university. Here, as in most colleges of education, he recounted, the instructors held that the research was against it. . . . When he asked *what* research, the principal said, no one was able to tell him.

Judging from what they told me, the education in the teaching of reading received by teachers, principals and supervisors generally acts as a force against experimentation and change.[4]

Anyone fortunate enough to have a good professor for *any* course ought to be happy. Most people I know find it hard to remember a few professors from the 40 or so they had been exposed to in college that had any great impact on them. It is sad, however, when reading teachers are exposed to only "one best way" when there are so many alternatives and different learning styles among children.

The only thing that most children with reading problems have in common is that they have not been taught to read. Reading is a complex task, but it does not take 10 years to master. A small percentage of children have special learning problems, but almost every child arrives at school with varied experiences and language to describe them. The fact that teachers of reading are often inadequately prepared technicians can be blamed directly on their experiences in teacher-education programs. They lack knowledge of the basic skills of reading and are dependent on a particular basal reader for a philosophy and approach to teaching. In addition, many teachers are ill-prepared to relate to today's children or to meet their needs, socially, emotionally, or educationally. Teacher preparation for urban schools is especially poor. If a teacher has the best training possible in reading, but cannot cope with children from different racial or ethnic groups, the teacher will most likely fail. Herbert Foster, author of *Ribbin', Jivin' and Playin' the Dozens: The Unrecognized Dilemma of Inner City Schools,*[5] blames the failure of urban teachers on teacher-education programs. He says, "The formal organizational rules set up by traditionalist teachers . . . relate to order in the classroom, quietness, things like that. However, the rules that are *really* running the school are the informal organizational rules created by lower-class black male street-corner behavior."[5] Because teacher-education institutions don't teach these phenomena, would-be good teachers fail in urban schools. For example, "playing the dozens" is a game played by lower-class blacks in which verbal ability is tested in a battle of insults. Strength and masculinity are shown by verbally putting down one's adversary. This street-corner game brought into the classroom and *not* understood by the teacher often causes unnecessary problems.

Criticism of teacher education certainly is not new. I don't think I've ever met a teacher or former teacher who didn't complain about "dull" education courses, especially in reading. There is pretty wide agreement among teachers that teacher-education institutions:

- produce incompetent teachers
- prepare mediocre college professors
- perpetuate bland materials
- perpetuate time-in-course standards for teacher certification
- reinforce the use of invalid tests
- disseminate shoddy research data
- treat theory as hard data
- engage in debates over theories
- favor emotions over hard data
- protect the status quo
- promote illiteracy

Many teachers are certified without ever taking a course in teaching reading. Virtually every state which has certification standards for reading specialists specifies *graduate*-level courses. Even the IRA's recommendations on certification specify graduate courses. Also, traditional graduate training courses in reading overlap tremendously in course content and usually ignore the teacher and the learner as human beings. Most elementary school teachers who have taken a reading course have been exposed to one three-credit "methods" course in the teaching of reading that probably looks something like this:

Format. Lecture, with 30 to 50 students in the class.

Requirements. Read the required textbook—the text will be either a book written by the professor's former professor or a book which has been used for years and is in its second or third edition (once a professor knows a book, has prepared exams for it, and has taught from it for years, he or she is, understandably, reluctant to change)—a midterm and final exam and a research paper.

Grading. The grade is based one-third each on the two exams and one-third on the paper. The exams cover the lectures and the textbook.

Procedures. The professor lectures 3 hours per week for approximately 15 weeks. The midterm exam covers the first 7 weeks of lectures, and the final exam covers the whole course. The research paper is to be written on one of the major topics for the course and can be no longer than 10 pages. (Sound familiar?)

Topics. The professor usually covers the same topics as the chapters in the text. The professor may digress to discuss the subject he or she is presently researching for the annual required publication or to cover a favorite topic. Here we see the major shortcoming of courses in how to teach reading—what the educators call the difference between theory and practice. Education courses are traditionally criticized because they are theory-oriented rather than practical. Although this is true, the problem goes even deeper. Prospective teachers do not learn or are not exposed to the feelings of kids and teachers or the negative aspects of school, what Postman and Weingartner[6] call "subversive activities." Prospective teachers are not required to teach real live children until their student teaching experience, which is usually in their senior year. At this point, if the student teacher cannot cope with "real-world" problems, it is too late. On page 56 is a list of topics usually covered in how-to-teach-reading courses wtih some "real-world" counterparts that usually are not discussed. These 17 points are included in a list of areas considered "essential for professional development in reading" by a group of 27 reading-teacher educators chosen to be part of a commission on "high-quality" teacher education in reading in 1974. They were assisted by 108 field consultants, who were also college or university reading-teacher educators.[7] Such lists are usually written in pedagese (language that only educators can understand) that is almost impossible to interpret. This one is no exception.

Another reason education courses are so bad is that each state has its own "mini" Reading Machine. The state branches of the national professional associations tend to reinforce interrelationships among the state education department, local colleges, and local school systems. For example, the federal "Right to Read" program has a "Right to Read" coordinator in every state but Hawaii. This coordinator serves as a liaison between the federal government and the state department of education. "Right to Read" has funded 31 of the states with grants totaling more than 4 million dollars to develop "Right to Read" staffs in local school districts. In practically every state, some existing leader of the school system reading programs was in some way paid to participate in a program to help end illiteracy. This is enlisting the aid of the problem to help solve the problem. The "Right to Read" program is offering more of the same old stuff.

An example of such inbreeding exists in the Boston area. At a meeting of the New England Reading Association in 1961, Donald

The Seventeen Essential Areas	Some Real-World Counterparts Not Usually Covered in Teacher-Education Courses (without the pedagese)
1. Understanding the English language as a communication system	1. Swearing and local slang. Nonverbal actions often communicate more than verbal.
2. Interaction with parents and the community	2. Militant parents are becoming more and more aware of how to change the schools.
3. Instructional planning: curriculum and approaches	3. Most beginning teachers have absolutely no power to choose the books they will use, or the instructional approach.
4. Developing language fluency and perceptual abilities in early childhood	4. By the time kids are in schools at age 6 and above, such abilities have been "developed" in 90 percent of them.
5. Continued language development in social settings	5. Street language used in schools gets kids in trouble. Kids learn more language from television than from school.
6. Teaching word-attack skills	6. This can be learned only by actually teaching real live kids.
7. Developing comprehension: analysis of meaning 8. Synthesis and generalization 9. Information acquisition	7, 8, 9. These are *thinking* skills kids use in their everyday life. There are never any correct answers when kids understand or "comprehend."
10. Developing literary appreciation: young children 11. Latency years 12. Young adults	10, 11, 12. Kids know what turns them on. Kids who have reading problems hate reading and school books.
13. Diagnostic evaluation of reading progress	13. Schools test kids to death at the expense of teaching them.
14. School and classroom organization for diagnostic teaching	14. Most learning takes place outside the four walls of a classroom.
15. Adapting instruction to varied linguistic backgrounds	15. A kid who speaks Spanish may know how to read Spanish perfectly well.
16. Treatment of special reading problems	16. Most kids with reading problems really have people (teacher) problems.
17. Initiating improvements in school programs	17. Young teachers who rock the boat get fired.

Durrell, then of Boston University, asked an audience of 500 administrators and reading teachers, "How many of you have taken courses with me at Boston University?" Nearly every teacher and administrator in the room raised his or her hand. Practically every reading specialist in the city had graduated from Boston University and had returned there to take in-service courses. (In-service courses are taken for course credits that teachers are required to accumulate to keep their certification.) Furthermore, most of the professors in the School of Education at Boston University had received their degrees there. Such inbreeding is not unusual in the reading field. If a director of reading in a college hires one of his own graduates, the graduate will be less likely to threaten or question the director's position.

When I took my first graduate course in the teaching of reading, the professor mentioned that reading-teacher conventions were nothing more than meetings of mutual admiration societies. I started attending conventions more than 15 years ago. They were heady experiences. I saw and heard the authors and famous reading authorities I had read and heard about. Since then I have come to understand that my first graduate professor was correct. I suspect it is as true today as it was then that the local teachers in the city where the conventions are held each year (they rotate around the country) are as awestruck as I was at actually seeing and hearing "leaders in reading" on stage at the local convention hall. In May 1975, the IRA's annual convention was held in New York City. Since New York State has the largest number of IRA members of any state with 3,086, I would guess that most of the more than 10,000 attendees at that conference were teachers visiting the fountain of the reading gods much as I was.

The IRA is not the only club of reading teachers, although it is the largest, with more than 65,000 members and over 68,000 subscribers to its publications. Other than the state and local organizations of reading people, the major reading professional organizations are:

- International Reading Association
- National Reading Conference
- National Council of Teachers of English
- College Reading Association
- New England Reading Association
- Midwest Reading Association

The IRA alone has a network of local councils all over the world. There are 45 state councils with 743 local councils. In other countries there are more than 49 additional councils, 23 of them in Canada. The IRA has been criticized by reading leaders overseas for not really being international. Ted Gloger based his doctoral dissertation at the University of Massachusetts on a year-long tour he took visiting leaders in reading and reading programs in 13 countries. Gloger stated that when he suggested that leaders in the various countries play an active role in the IRA, "They would smile and say, 'You mean the American Reading Association!' "[8] In attempting to be more "international," the IRA opened an office in Paris in 1974.

Since I have been involved with reading organizations for over 15 years, I have become less awestruck. (I was on the board of directors of the College Reading Association [CRA], chairman of the Professional Standards and Ethics Committee, and a member of the editorial advisory committee of the IRA's *The Reading Teacher* and have spoken at one of the conventions nearly every year for the past 8 years.) These organizations meet annually in various parts of the country for the members to find jobs, meet old friends, get away for a vacation, and, most importantly, advance professionally, both within the educational area and in the member's own college or university. As institutions of higher learning use publishing as a criterion in their reward systems, so do they use participation in national conventions as an indication of competence. As a result of this system, conventions sometimes have more people as speakers, introducers, chairmen, and reactors, than they have in the audience. (Participation in a convention often means that the professor or teacher will be paid for travel to the convention.) As one can imagine, the convention programs are lengthy indeed. At the IRA's 1973 convention in Denver, there were 828 participants or speakers. The program booklet alone was 110 pages long. At the 1974 convention in New Orleans, the number of speakers increased to 1,211; in New York in 1975, the number was 1,234. Since more than 10,000 people attend each IRA convention, it will be quite a while before the number of speakers outnumbers the participants, but at a recent annual convention of the CRA, no more than an average of 10 people attended each meeting; there were 84 people on the program. There is now a rule in the IRA that one can only be on the program for one talk, but this only serves to maximize the number of people who can be rewarded by a slot on the program.

Conventions are also where publishers show their wares. There were 170 exhibits at the Denver convention, 145 at the New Orleans convention, and, of course, 211 in New York. These conventions are the only places where the publishers come into direct contact with large numbers of reading professors and reading teachers. Elaborate cocktail parties and sales pitches take place. Some of the exhibits take on the aura of state fair sideshows while others look like Fifth Avenue salons. The enormous amount of money to be made in the reading business promotes fierce competition among the businessmen.

Such associations have great power and influence over policies and standards within the profession. I have seen more perpetuation of status-quo, don't-rock-the-boat, and keep-things-the-way-they-are activities in reading organizations than I have in any other. It is virtually impossible to get a positive vote on an innovative, exciting idea at meetings of the boards of directors of these organizations if it is perceived as threatening by the members. Self-protection, self-congratulation, and self-perpetuation are the rules. Of course, this is one of the purposes of institutions like the IRA. This is not to say that such organizations do not promote positive programs: They also lobby for teacher licensing procedures in the states, promote reading programs, and support federal programs such as the "Right to Read" and television programs like "Sesame Street" and "The Electric Company."

One author, not a reading professional, has observed that the IRA is a devious organization which exists to preserve the "whole-word" method of teaching reading. In a book which is clearly an emotion-laden appeal to get schools and teachers back to phonics, Samuel Blumenfeld observed:

> The most powerful lobby in the United States for the whole-word method is the International Reading Association . . . the leadership of the I.R.A. was composed of the authors of America's best-selling whole-word basal reading programs. They had gathered together not only to defend their professional interests but their considerable economic interests as well. That is what is known as the institutionalization of vested interests. It is as simple as that.[9]

The topics discussed at meetings of professional reading organizations is the professional journal—the outlet for teacher educaphasizes excellence in teaching reading, presumably for the benefit of classroom teachers. Following are some of the topics that were discussed at the conference of the CRA in Maryland in 1974:

- Instant diagnosis: using oral reading miscues to identify specific problems and prescribe remediation
- Revised Harris-Jacobsen readability formulas
- The leadership characteristics of female teachers and non-teachers by socio–economic status.
- Short-term memory and reading-related language patterns

It is understandable that there were only an average of 10 people in each speaker's audience.

Cocktail parties, renewing old acquaintances, and a chance to travel—these are the reasons reading educators go to annual meetings of professional organizations. The actual business of professional reading organizations is carried on by salaried, full-time executive secretaries or directors.

Another reason for the existence of professional reading organizations is the professional journal—the outlet for teacher educators who are trapped in the publish-or-perish bind at colleges and universities. One organization's journal—the CRA's *Reading World*—is an excellent example of how an organization's board of directors not only protects the status quo, but its own publishing interests as well. In perusing the eight issues of *Reading World* from October 1972 to May 1974 (it is published quarterly), I found that at least one member of the board of directors or a former president of the organization appeared as an author in all but one issue. Faculty members from the editor's college appeared in three of the issues.

When graduate students are working on advanced degrees (an Ed.D. or Ph.D. in education), they usually support themselves by taking jobs as research assistants or teaching assistants. A research assistant gathers information for research studies, such as testing children in schools or helping teachers test new materials, etc. A teaching assistant either actually teaches one or two how-to-teach-reading courses or helps the professor conduct an advanced course by grading his papers. At any rate, in both jobs, the major professor is the boss. Furthermore, doctoral students become very dependent on the major professor for survival in graduate school. The major professor or chairperson of the doctoral committee is the one person who facilitates the final completion of the degree for the doctoral student. The chairperson of the doctoral committee directs the work on the doctoral dissertation. If the dissertation is poor, it reflects as much on the chairperson as it does on the student. So the chairperson becomes a god and a taskmaster. Having been so dependent on one person for so long (the average doctoral program takes 5 to 6 years to complete), when the student is hired by the former chairperson, the inferiority and dependency are very difficult to shed. When a director of a reading program begins to hire his or her own graduates, to publish textbooks and basal-reader series, to publish books dealing with his or her own research, and to develop a reputation as head of a major center for training reading teachers in the area, an empire is in the making, with a single professor–author–mentor at the top. The "mentorship" passes on as the leaders grow old and retire, but the ideas, books, and techniques of the mentor are passed on, safely guarded from change.

People train to be professors of reading by being doctoral candidates. In universities of over 10,000 students, the major training vehicle for doctoral students learning how to teach is their assignment to teach one of the undergraduate how-to-teach-reading courses or to supervise some student teachers in the schools. A graduate-student teaching assistant certainly receives no training in teaching. It is assumed that since doctoral students have most likely taught in elementary or secondary schools (but many have absolutely no such experience!), they are competent to teach undergraduates. For the doctoral student, teaching the undergraduate course is a sink-or-swim proposition. Most are thankful for the chance to get the experience. An examination of the curricula of most doctoral programs in reading indicates a heavy emphasis on reading theory and research and absolutely no content on undergraduate teacher-education approaches, how to teach college students, alternative means of presenting information, or how to facilitate practical experiences in teaching reading to children. Doctoral students are *forced* into teaching the how-to-teach-reading course as they were taught it when they were undergraduates, perpetuating the dull lecture, text, test courses of the past, because they most often have little or no practical experience to draw on.

Given this situation in teacher-education programs, it is easy to understand why better than 95 percent of the classrooms in this country use graded basal readers as the major means of teaching reading. My own son and daughter, who attended an elementary school in a supposedly progressive, middle-class suburban school system with a good reputation, were exposed to the 1962 revision of the *Scott, Foresman Readers* (originally published in 1912) from 1972 to 1975. These readers are the old Dick and Jane readers that have received so much negative publicity for their bland, racist, sexist content.[10] In 1970, Scott, Foresman executives were so embarrassed by Dick and Jane that they announced in *The New York Times* and elsewhere that the old readers were obsolete with the publication of Scott, Foresman's new *System 70s* readers. Well, until 1975 Dick and Jane were very much alive in East Grand Rapids, Mich., and in thousands of other school systems across the country that either couldn't afford to replace the old readers or had teachers who "taught hundreds of children to read with Dick and Jane, and if it worked with them, it will work for the children of the 1970s." Not all children are deprived by having to read these readers. Young children who are excited about learning to read will learn regardless of *what* they read; the exciting thing is that they are *reading*. The pity is that there are so many other, newer, more imaginative, realistic, and exciting materials available. Look at any publisher's catalogue for examples. I find it hard to believe that a school system that spends an average of more than $150 per child per year can't afford to use the best materials available. It makes one wonder just what the economic priorities are. In many schools, budget allocations for athletics, tennis courts, and administrator salaries are actually higher than for the reading program.

The major reason for the widespread use of basal readers is, of course, that they are so easy to use. You could hand any high school graduate a teacher's manual and make that person a reading teacher in 1 day. The manuals spell it out in boldfaced type: "**Now ask the children, 'Have you ever had a new dog?'**" Teachers are led to believe that if they follow the instructions in the teacher's manual, they are teaching reading. They believe that if children read through reader after reader and complete the accompanying workbooks, they have mastered the skills of reading. Finally, they actually believe that graded basal readers were scientifically developed and include some kind of magic that will do the job for them, and they insist on "covering" the book during the year. (I recently heard an extremely successful director of reading say she tells her teachers that, if they want to "cover" a basal reader, "sit on it!")

I have described teacher education in reading as a sad state of affairs. I don't want to leave this topic without saying that we do have quite a bit of information about good teaching, good teacher-education programs, and alternative means of facilitating learning to read. Arthur Combs, a teacher educator at the University of Florida, has identified the major problem in teacher-education programs. Teacher education, he says, "has been successful in gathering information and in making information available to students. . . . We are experts at telling people what they need to know, and we measure the success of teaching by requiring students to tell it back to us." Essential for teacher-education programs, he continues, "is helping people to discover the personal meaning of information so that they *behave* differently as a result of teaching."[11] Memorizing information so it can be spewed forth on a test and promptly forgotten the next day, a process that so many teachers have gone through during their college years, is clearly a teacher-education program of the nineteenth century.

It would be impossible to cite the attributes of a good reading teacher and have them apply to all teachers in all situations. A good reading teacher in Westport, Conn., or Hillsborough, Calif., may very well not be a good reading teacher in the Watts section of Los Angeles or in the Ocean Hill-Brownsville section of New York City. Still, I feel teacher-education institutions are moving in the right direction, albeit slowly. In a recent study of teacher-selection criteria, Marti Yarington and Horace Reed, of the University of Massachusetts, analyzed the subjective opinions of a cross section of educators regarding the competencies or attitudes most important for successful teaching. Through interviews with faculty and graduate students in education, they developed the following list[12] of what a competent teacher is:

1. sensitive
2. unbiased
3. flexible
4. concerned with children's growth
5. self-aware
6. enthusiastic
7. warm
8. honest

Furthermore, a competent teacher has:

1. a broad range of experience
2. a sense of humor
3. a strong self-concept
4. a desire to teach

The behavioral descriptions of the above traits can be found in the Appendix.

As an alternative to quantitative criteria or in-course means of certifying reading teachers, qualitative criteria can be demanded by requiring prospective reading teachers to meet certain agreed-upon, specific competencies. A list of such competencies could be the minimum standards by which reading teachers would be judged. I recently directed a curriculum development project at Aquinas College under a grant from the USOE.[13] We developed 14 competency-based courses to train classroom reading specialists. Each course had a list of competencies the prospective teachers had to meet. Under each competency were listed the performances with kids, the knowledge, and the attitudes required to meet the competency. Following are the topics of the 14 courses:

1. Reading/Language Arts, K–12
2. Readiness and Beginning Reading
3. Comprehension
4. Diagnosis
5. Learning/Study Styles
6. The Future: Trial/Error Teaching/Learning
7. Administration and Supervision
8. Remediation and Clinical Practicum
9. The Affective Domain
10. Process—Theory and Practice
11. Research and Measurement
12. Survival Skills
13. Presentation Skills
14. Sexism and Racism

One can imagine the difficulty in hiring teachers that meet the above criteria when the only evidence teachers present is a transcript of courses completed. However, the direction for the future is clear. As school enrollments continue to go down and as the need for teachers subsides even more, school systems will demand more and more accountability from their teachers. They will not be hired unless they meet unique competencies like the ones covered under the topics above. It will not be enough to have graduated from a teacher-education institution. New teachers will be forced to demonstrate that they are competent—as teachers and as human beings.

In a study conducted in the Portland, Ore., public schools,[14] Eaton Conant found that teachers spent only 30 percent of their time in activities related to academic instruction—100 minutes out of a 5½-hour day. Seventy-five minutes were devoted to language arts (reading), 18 to math, and no more than 1 or 2 minutes daily to any other curriculum area. Less than an hour per day was spent in individual or small-group teaching—2 minutes per child in a class of 25. It is not that teachers do nothing else: Their teacher-education programs offered little constructive training in specific instructional activities, so it is easier for the teachers to spend time doing what they know well—collecting milk money, disciplining kids, and babysitting.

There is good reason to believe that change in teacher education will take place. After years of trying to change schools by radical innovation, new materials and techniques, and the like, educators have learned that schools are people. Schools are cultures unto themselves. Seymour Sarason, in *The Culture of the School and the Problem of Change*,[15] says that schools will never be changed until one fully understands the culture of the individual school one is trying to change, as a group of unique human beings. There is no reason to believe that teacher-education institutions should not be treated the same way.

No one would deny that our American society has changed more rapidly during the late 1960s and early 1970s than at any other time in history. There is a new call for change in education that is working, not because of change for change's sake, and not because of radical innovators, but because society itself is changing, and people are demanding change. Sidney Marland, Jr., former assistant secretary of education in HEW, said that the people who need change "are not attacking our fortress (education) at all. They're just detouring around it because so many of them, including students, don't think we guard anything worth taking."[16] Fewer and fewer students are attending colleges today because what the colleges offer is not needed to survive in today's society. It was reported that average verbal scores on the college boards, the Scholastic Aptitude Tests (SATs) that high school students take for college admission, are declining (in 1956 and 1957 the average was 473; in 1969 and 1970 it had declined to 461 and has continued to decline since). Gene Hawes, author of the report, suggested "that these abilities as assayed by the tests may come to mean less and less in college admission with rising social and cultural change."[17] SAT scores are losing value in today's society, so much so that we hear much more today about college "recruiting" than we do about college "admissions."

Dean Corrigan, dean of the College of Education at the University of Maryland, said, "Memorizing detailed information and didactic material passed on to them by the older generation before they confront real teaching tasks is useless." He said teacher-education students will only learn by "having the opportunity to make choices and deal with consequences."[18]

Today's new teacher-education programs, whether they be humanistic, competency based, or public school based, are certainly better than the old lecture–textbook–paper–test courses. The question is: How soon will *all* of our colleges and universities recognize that fact?

References

1. Austin, Mary C., and Morrison, Coleman, *The Torch Lighters, Tomorrow's Teachers of Reading,* Harvard University Press, Cambridge, Mass., 1961.
2. Rickover, H. G., *Swiss Schools and Ours: Why Theirs Are Better,* Little, Brown and Co., Boston, 1962, p. 7.
3. Otto, Wayne, and Dulin, Kenneth, "How to Succeed in Reading by Really Trying," in *Reading: Process and Pedagogy, 19th Yearbook of the National Reading Conference,* vol. 2, 1970, pp. 134–141.
4. Chall, Jeanne S., *Learning to Read: The Great Debate,* McGraw-Hill Book Co., New York, 1967, p. 296.
5. Foster, Herbert, *Ribbin', Jivin', and Playin' the Dozens: The Unrecognized Dilemma of Inner City Schools,* Ballinger Publishing Co., Cambridge, Mass., 1974.
6. Postman, Neil, and Weingartner, Charles, *Teaching as a Subversive Activity,* Dell Books, New York, 1971.
7. Sartain, Harry, and Stanton, Paul (editors), *Modular Preparation for Teaching Reading,* International Reading Association, Newark, Del., 1974, pp. 32–33.
8. Gloger, Maxwell T., "An Observation of Reading Programs within Selected Countries around the World," unpublished doctoral dissertation, University of Massachusetts, Amherst, Mass., 1975.

9. Blumenfeld, Samuel L., *The New Illiterates and How to Keep Your Child from Becoming One*, Arlington House, New Rochelle, N.Y., 1973, pp. 120–121.

10. *Dick and Jane as Victims, Sex Stereotyping in Children's Readers*, Women on Words & Images, Princeton, N.J., 1972.

11. Combs, Arthur, et al., *The Professional Education of Teachers*, 2nd edition, Allyn and Bacon, Inc., Boston, 1974, p. 31.

12. Yarington, Marti, and Reed, Horace, "A Procedure for Establishing Teacher Education Criteria," *Journal of the Student Personnel Association for Teacher Education*, vol. 12, March 1974, pp. 109–113.

13. Yarington, David J., *Classroom Reading Specialist Program*, USOE Grant No. OEG-0-74-8981, Year End Report, 4 volumes, 1975, 742 p.

14. Conant, Eaton H., "What Do Teachers Do All Day," *Saturday Review/World*, vol. 1, June 1, 1974, p. 55.

15. Sarason, Seymour B., *The Culture of the School and the Problem of Change*, Allyn and Bacon, Inc., Boston, 1971.

16. Marland, Sidney, Jr., "Career Education" paper given at the annual conference of the National Council of Teachers of English, November 24, 1972.

17. Hawes, Gene, "The Decline of the SATs," *Change*, vol. 4, November 1972, p. 17.

18. Corrigan, Dean C., "Underlying Premises for Learner-Centered Competency-Based Teacher Education," PBTE, Multi-State Consortium on Performance-Based Teacher Education, vol. 3, No. 3, September 1974, p. 6.

SIX

RACISM, CENSORSHIP, AND SEXISM*

"All right, now, let's settle down and try our assignment . . . *The House of the Seven Gables.* First row, first seat. Ellis. Start at the beginning, please. Read until I tell you to stop."

Junebug got to his feet and started to riffle the pages. He clowned with the book upside down, then opened it at the back. The kids close by giggled.

"First page, Ellis, first line, first sentence, first word. . . ."

Junebug turned to the title page and began to read, *"The House of the Seven Gables,* by Nathaniel Hawthorne."

"Yes, I think we've established that, Mr. Ellis."

Unable to stall any more, Junebug began to read, slowly, hesitantly, like a fourth or fifth grader. "Half way down a by-street of one of our New England towns stands a ru-ru—ru. . . ."

"Rusty."

"Rusty wooden house, with seven ac . . . acurate . . ."

"Acutely."

". . . acute-ly p . . . pe . . ."

"Peaked."

". . . peaked ga . . . gables, facing towards var . . . var . . ." Junebug was sweating, embarrassed. Quincy didn't look at him. He'd heard about reading problems in ghetto schools, but it was another thing to see it. To see a sharp street kid who was undoubtedly hip to the ways of the world fumbling over elementary school words. He let Ellis off the hook.

---

*This chapter is an expanded version of "Racism and the Reading Teacher," in *Reading Teachers for Urban Schools: New Attitudes, Improved Skills,* by David Yarington and Richard Schaye. It was a publication of the School of Education Center for Urban Education, *Career Opportunities Research Memoranda* Series, No. 14, University of Massachusetts, Amherst, Mass., May 1972.

"Thanks, Ellis. We'll have to work on it. Next."

Mae Marshall got up and nervously cleared her throat. "Where . . . sh . . . where should I start from?" She too was stalling for time.

"Where Ellis left off, Mae."

". . . facing towards var-i-ous points of the compass. The street is Pinch . . . Pinn . . ." She looked up, embarrassed and shook her head.

"Pyncheon Street, Mae."

"Pyncheon Street." Then she backtracked as a child will to remember where a letter sits in the alphabet. "The street was Pyn-che-on Street and the house is the old Pynchin house, and an elm tree of wide kermfroms. . . ."

"Circumference." Like a parent, Quincy wanted to take it away from the kids and do it for them. It was too painful. But he knew that wouldn't help. He had to know the depth of the difficulty here . . . you couldn't expect the kids to jump the hurdles before they'd learned to walk.

Mae went on. ". . . of wide circumference, rotted. . . ."

"Rooted."

". . . of wide circumference, rooted before the door, is fame. . . ."

"Familiar . . ."

Mae looked up. The tough, self-assured girl who'd commandeered Sherry Vaughn's seat yesterday had tears in her eyes. She wanted to be saved from the ordeal.

"All right, Mae. Thank you."

The girl flopped back into her seat wiping the damp wisps of hair from her forehead.

"Johnson."

Johnson remained slouched in his chair. His usually bright expression had dulled into boredom. He made no move to get up.

"Johnson," Quincy repeated.

Johnson got up, muttering to himself.

"I'm sorry, Johnson, I didn't hear you."

"I said, so far this is one hell of a story."

Quincy felt inclined to agree. He gave Johnson a look. The kid began to read.

"The as . . . a . . . ass. . . ."

"The aspect."

Johnson didn't repeat the proferred word, just continued on with the next one. ". . . of the nev . . . vener. . . ."

"Venerable mansion."

". . . . has always affected me like a hu-man. . . ."

Quincy presupposed that Johnson would have difficulty with the next word. He forestalled him. "Countenance . . . Johnson, did you prepare this last night?" The kid nodded his head rapidly, three or four times. Quincy was convinced he was protesting too much. "Hmmm. . . . Okay. That'll do." He made a note, not looking to see who the next reader was, just automatically, a little wearily, said, "Next."

"Were these to be worthily recounted, they would form a narrative of no small interest and instruction. . . ."

Quincy looked up, thrown by the unexpected fluency, the intelligent reading. It was Doug. Quincy relaxed slightly, hoping the apparent ease of the white kid's reading might spark an interest in the narrative. There was a rustle in the classroom, a chill, soundless sound. Quincy looked around. The faces of the black kids made a visible statement of their hurt, their resentment at being shown up. No kid looked at another. No whisper, no movement, no physical contact, yet a message had been sent. The hostility in the room was as tangible a presence as the thirty black kids sitting there. Most of them were as vulnerable in their demonstrated inadequacy as a soldier without a weapon confronted by a hated, armed attacker.

" . . . and possessing, moreover, a certain remarkable unity which might almost seem the result of artistic arrangement." Doug went on, self-confident, flaunting his obvious ease against the black kids' feelings of inferiority.

Quincy, realizing his mistake, rushed in to right it. "That's enough. Thank you . . . we'll . . . uh . . . go to something else." Doug sat down. The silence in the room bore down on Quincy, registering in his tense shoulder muscles. He shuffled some papers on his desk, trying to think of some way of diverting the kids' attention. Fortunately, just then the bell rang. The kids filed silently out of the room, leaving behind a shaken Quincy.[1]

Racism

Classroom reading problems such as the above often are compounded by friction between black and white students. Reading specialists are fond of saying that every teacher is a reading teacher and that teachers in elementary schools and high school English teachers know how to teach reading. Nothing is farther from the truth. If it were so, middle school, junior high, and high school students with reading problems would have learned to read in elementary school. If it were so, secondary school teachers could facilitate their learning to read, rather than expecting a high level of performance in reading a specific subject with no regard for students' reading abilities. Schools would be making great progress if every teacher who is expected to be a reading teacher was.

There are a variety of theories as to why children in urban schools generally read so poorly. Most of these theories focus on problems of the child rather than problems of the school. The difficulty with these theories is their failure to account for the children who are proficient readers and yet in all other variables are similar to those children who are nonreaders.

The most plausible reason for reading failure in urban schools is the impact of racism on minority children. Racism obviously encompasses more than the attitudes of teachers and other school personnel—but these particular attitudes are crucial to the child's reading environment. It is difficult to pin down the insidious nature of racism, however. The literature on urban education is devoted to factors other than school and teacher prejudices and expectations. Most of the research scrutinizes the victim—a racist tactic in itself.

Reading failure in urban schools is well documented. Let's examine some of the more important data.

Reading failure does not fall equally on all groups in our society. Blacks, as a group, and inner-city youth, including many other minority groups, consistently score lower than whites on reading achievement. This has been dramatically revealed in the data gathered in the National Assessment of Educational Progress (NAEP) project described earlier. NAEP reaffirmed what several other studies on black achievement have said all along: that minority groups, blacks in particular, are discriminated against in the teaching of reading in the United States. Donald Gallo, professor of English at Central Connecticut State College and author of the NAEP report, stated:

> Poor performance by Blacks on the National Reading Assessment is a harsh reality, a reality that reflects the position of Blacks in American society in 1970–71. In no skills area (theme) assessed in this study did Blacks approach the national level. And on only 16 of the more than 700 exercises did Blacks read at or slightly above the national level.
>
> That does not mean that the reading skills of all Blacks are inferior to all Whites or that an individual Black person can be expected to read less well than an individual White person

from a comparable background. It does mean, however, that Whites as a group consistently perform better than Blacks as a group on various measures of a variety of reading skills.[2]

That same report discussed the reactions of six reading "experts" to the data. I stated at that time:

> "This research report seems to me to be doing the same thing that all studies (on Blacks) have done for years," he said, "and that is blame failure on kids. All the way through, this study asks, 'Why do these kids do poorly? Why do these kids do so and so?' And it seems to me that the one thing that all these poor readers have in common—Black kids in particular—is that they have not been *taught* to read. I see it as the failure of schools and teachers to teach reading."[3]

On July 27, 1967, President Johnson appointed a commission, chaired by Otto Kerner,[4] to study the causes of the riots in cities all over the country that year, primarily the riots in Newark and Detroit. In 1968 the Kerner Commission reported that black students in the metropolitan northeast were, on the average, 1.6 grades behind the national level. In the same report, Kenneth Clark clearly stated the problem of teacher attitudes:

> . . . the answer to the question of the best way to teach "the disadvantaged" is embarrassingly simple—namely to teach them with the same expectations, the same acceptance of their humanity and their educability and, therefore, with the same effectiveness as one would teach the more privileged child.[5]

There are some studies that focus on teacher attitudes. William Woodworth and Richard Salzer[6] used a tape recording of a black child and a white child each reading the same passage to test the attitudes of 119 teachers toward the children. Their study concluded that the teachers identified the black child's voice with his racial background, and that the teachers associated such a background with negative achievement expectations. Frederick Williams[7] found that teachers listening to tapes of black and white children made judgments about the status of the children based on whether they spoke standard or nonstandard English. Ray Rist conducted a study of how children are grouped for reading instruction in the beginning grades.[8] He documented the importance of teacher expectations, both in placing children in fast and slow reading groups and in keeping them there. Eleanor Leacock[9] observed a number of teachers in city schools and discovered that many teachers were unwilling to impose "middle-class goals" on low-income black children because they said these goals were unrealistic for the children. These teachers frequently defined the low-income black children as inadequate and their proper role as one of deference. It is clear from these studies that teacher attitudes toward both race and class determine their expectations for the child. Unfortunately, there is little available data which distinguishes between racial and class prejudice, although the two are clearly intertwined.

In 1973, the U.S. Commission on Civil Rights published a study that revealed differences in teacher interaction with Mexican-American and Anglo (non-Mexican-American) students.[10] There is no reason to believe that the results would be any different were the study done with black, Puerto Rican, Cuban, Indian, or other minority-group children. The Commission on Civil Rights study was completed in the three southwest states with the largest number of Mexican-Americans—in California, New Mexico, and Texas. The data were collected in 494 classrooms in 430 different schools using a technique called Flanders Interaction Analysis, a classroom observation check-off system which codes classroom teacher behavior every 3 seconds according to the following 10 categories:

1. Teacher accepts students' feelings.
2. Teacher praises student.
3. Teacher accepts or uses students' ideas.
4. Teacher asks a question.
5. Teacher lectures.
6. Teacher gives student directions.
7. Teacher criticizes student.
8. Student speaks in response to teacher's question or directions.
9. Student speaks on his own initiative.
10. No one is speaking or confusion prevails.[11]

The U.S. Commission on Civil Rights study reports the following six significant differences between teacher attitudes toward Chicano (Mexican-American) and Anglo children.

Disparities in teacher praise and encouragement. "The average Anglo received about 36 percent more praise or encouragement than the average Mexican-American pupil in the same classroom."

> Observation: One teacher, working in a predominantly Mexican-American school complained to Commission staff of the problem she faced: "I am a good teacher, I think. And if I had a normal bunch of kids I could teach. But this certainly is not a normal bunch of kids."[12]

Acceptance and use of student ideas. "The average Anglo pupil in the survey area hears the teacher repeat, or refer to, an idea he or she has expressed about 40 percent more than does the average Chicano pupil"[13]

Positive teacher response. "The average Anglo pupil receives about 40 percent more positive response from the teacher than does the average Chicano pupil."[14]

Teacher questioning. "The average Anglo pupil in the survey area receives about 21 percent more questioning from the teacher than the average Chicano pupil."[15]

All noncriticizing talk by the teacher. "Teachers spend 23 percent more time in all nondisapproving talk with Anglo than with Chicano pupils."

> Observation: Mrs. M. was leading a class discussion on unions, but all the interaction was between the teacher and three Anglos sitting in the front of the class. They were very eager, but the rest of the class was bored. Mrs. M. finally said: "The same hands, I always see the same hands."[16]

All student speaking. "The average Anglo student spends about 27 percent more time speaking in the classroom than the average Chicano student."

> Observation: One Chicano sat toward the back in a corner and volunteered several answers. At one point the teacher did not even acknowledge, much less reinforce, his answer. At another time he volunteered an answer which was perfectly suitable. Yet the teacher stated: "Well, yes, uh huh, but can anyone else put it in different terms?" The teacher then called on an Anglo boy who gave the same basic response with very little paraphrasing. The teacher then beamed and exclaimed: "Yes, that's it exactly."[17]

Legislation and court decisions requiring integration in school systems where races have been segregated have revealed that racism in northern school systems appears to be even stronger than in the South. The Boston experiences in the 1970s provided a good example. White South Boston residents were so adamantly opposed to integrating their schools that racial fights, demonstrations against busing, and closed schools were the norm for a long time. However, that should not lead us to believe that the South no longer uses racist tactics in schools. I visited a "liberal" school system in Mississippi which had recently been integrated according to federal guidelines. I walked into one elementary classroom just as the teacher was dividing the children into the traditional three reading groups. There were 25 children in the second-grade classroom. Seven were black and 18 were white. The teacher was saying, as I entered the room, "All right, the Bluebirds over here, the Robins at the table, and the Sparrows in the corner." Sure enough, the Sparrows group included the seven black children, no whites. The other two groups included all the white children. When I asked the teacher why, she stated that she couldn't help it if the low group contained all black kids—it wasn't her fault. I'll never know whether it was or wasn't. But it occurred to me that this might be one way to defy the integration laws within the self-contained classroom.

Another way that racism can be perpetuated in reading classrooms is by denigrating the way children have learned to speak; black dialect is an example. There is a debate among educators as to whether to accept black dialect as a legitimate means of communication or to force children to learn "standard English." The debate is over whether "different" is "wrong." Jan Torrey, a psychology professor at Connecticut College, explained the problem:

> For those learning to read, the implications of dialect differences can affect two quite different aspects of language. First, the differences between the Afro-American and standard dialects—in their phonological, grammatical and semantic structures—might lead to confusion and misunderstanding, complicating the already difficult reading process. Second, the cultural and personal functions of language and language differences might affect the social relations between a child and his school in such a way as to block effective learning. It is the thesis of this paper that the functional aspects of language have more serious implications for illiteracy than the structural ones. These functional aspects are closely connected with the conditions of life that keep people out of schools and the conditions of schools that keep people from learning to read in spite of ostensible efforts to teach them.
>
> Although standard English serves as the medium of instruction in reading and other subjects and is the only dialect accepted as "correct" in the dominant society, the deviations of many black children from the standard forms cannot be regarded as errors. These so-called "errors" actually conform to discernible grammatical rules, different from those of the standard language, but no less systematic. Furthermore, the patterns of black children's grammar that strike the standard English-speaking teacher as incomplete, illogical or linguistically retarded actually conform closely to rules of adult language spoken in the ghetto environment.[18]

The reason so few studies exist on the effects of teacher attitudes on learning to read is that the logistics of such a study are difficult. Researchers tend to probe where they can isolate variables easily. It is far easier to study unsuspecting children than school personnel. What school system is going to allow its personnel to be scrutinized on the subject of racial prejudice—the very prejudice which prevented anyone from accepting the conclusions of the U.S. Commission on Civil Rights? As Ronald G. Corwin stated in his study of class, status, and power in the public schools:

> . . . Persons who expect the schools to eliminate the problems of racial prejudice . . . ignore the important fact that schools traditionally have been places where such attitudes were reinforced. . . . The schools are part of society, nor apart from it; and as a result, the beliefs of those in control of society find their way into the classroom.[19]

Racism shows up not only in teacher attitudes but in the traditional reading program as well. We have been aware for many years that standarized reading tests and group intelligence tests were written for white, middle-class children. Even so, we continue to use these tests, and thereby penalize children for whom they were not devised. The result is to consign a large proportion of minority children to special education and remedial reading classrooms where little or no teaching occurs.

It takes very little research to unearth examples of these unfair, racist tests. One individually administered intelligence test, often used with children who are "nonverbal" or "nonreaders," is the *Peabody Picture Vocabulary Test.*[20] In this test, the child is asked to identify pictures. In one part of the test, the child is shown four pictures (a military cadet, a matador, a college graduate, and a porter). The child is told the word "porter" and asked to point to the porter. The point is not just that the porter is the only black, but that his job is also such a contrast with the three alternatives, all highly respected figures.

In my correspondence with the author of this test, he informed me (November 1, 1971)[21] that he didn't believe the illustrator was consciously racist; nor do I believe the author to have consciously placed that page in the test to be demeaning to blacks. But that is not the issue. The president of the publishing company informed me (October 1, 1971)[22] that the test was being revised. This test has been widely used since 1959. Once purchased, it is doubtful that it will be replaced by the revised version. In this case, schools perpetuate racist attitudes, unconsciously and through no overt or covert intention of the author, the publisher, or the teachers who use the test.

In teaching prospective teachers about the cultural unfairness of intelligence tests, I find it helpful to administer to them a test developed by Adrian Dove, a former Watts social worker, called *The Dove Counterbalance Intelligence Test.*[23] I first have the students view a videotaped demonstration of a traditional intelligence test laden with middle-class values and culture and designed for upper-middle-class white Anglo-Saxon Protestant children. They notice the various biases and prejudices present in the test. Then I administer the Dove test to the students, the majority of whom are white and middle class. The Dove test has such questions as:

> Cheap "chitlins" (not the kind you purchase at a frozen food counter) will taste rubbery unless they are cooked long enough. How soon do you quit cooking them to eat and enjoy them? a) 15 minutes, b) 2 hours, c) 24 hours, d) 1 week (on a low flame), e) one hour.

It is within the range of general knowledge of most black adults that the right answer is 24 hours. However, most whites have no knowledge of "chitlins" (chitterlings, the small intestines of pigs), much less how to cook them! My white students' low scores on the Dove test shock them into an awareness that tests can discriminate against people from different cultures.

Even more responsible than standardized tests for perpetuating nonachievement among minorities are the graded basal readers in use in 95 percent of our elementary schools. Traditionally these "Dick and Jane" stories have been about blonde-haired, blue-eyed children. During the 1960s, "ethnic" readers appeared with "Dick and Jane" colored brown. More sophisticated ethnic readers depicted actual black children but with the same story, set in middle-class suburbia. Jeanne Chall, in a large study of school readers, stated:

> While there is agitation for change in schools serving both the culturally and the economically advantaged and disadvantaged, the middle socio-economic group seems to remain quite satisfied with the *status quo.* Perhaps this is because this group is precisely the one for whom the existing basal-reading programs were devised and are most appropriate. The suburban middle-class child—not too affluent, and doing the ordinary things that all ordinary children in America do—can identify with Ted and Sally, Dick and Jane, Alice and Jerry, and the other heroes and heroines of the conventional basal readers. These readers are probably most suitable for this middle group; the pacing is not too taxing, and the questions they ask can be answered from the children's previous home experience.[24]

Publishers are beginning to respond, but some of the hastily prepared adoptions of programs that seem to offer quick solutions have content which is racist in nature. One example is a program called *Distar*,[25] which was specifically designed for disadvantaged children. Used widely in federal and public programs in almost every state, the *Distar* program was discovered to contain content of a demeaning and racist nature. *Distar* is one of the programs most widely used in "Follow Through," a federally funded program with 170 projects in communities across the country designed to follow up "Head Start." At least 19 of these projects have used the *Distar* materials in grades kindergarten through 3. *Distar* enjoyed immense popularity and was a financial success for its authors and publisher. In 1970, a group of parents, teachers, and school administrators in the Grand Rapids, Michigan, "Follow Through" program began to complain about the demeaning nature of some of the stories and illustrations in the *Distar* Level III reading materials. Since a majority of the children using the materials in the Grand Rapids project were black, it was disturbing to the parents to find that the Level III materials demeaned blacks. There were pictures of a black man called "boss" who jumped up and down and screamed when he got mad. When it was suggested to Mr. Engelmann that he revise the material, he refused because the materials had been published and were being used all over the country. It wasn't until several meetings had taken place, letters had been written back and forth, federal officials had been contacted, a 30-page list of proposed revisions had been written, and 3 years of negotiating, that Engelmann and his associates agreed to revise the program just for the Grand Rapids project. The nationally published materials remain the same. In January 1973, an article was published about Engelmann and *Distar* by Diane Divoky, a writer for *Learning* magazine. She described Engelmann as an "iconoclast with a no-nonsense mind. . . . He discarded all the conventional wisdom and hand-wringing and went about systematically figuring out answers." It is not surprising that Engelmann's unhappiness with the Grand Rapids "Follow Through" project comes through in the article:

> Then a tape of a Grand Rapids, Michigan, teacher comes on. The lesson is ragged and lackluster, the kids' voices uncertain. Engelmann's face falls. "What's that broad's name? She's really bad. She's a loser. That one kid leads all over the place, and one's behind. She should have stopped them right there and asked questions. There's no way she should have gone on. She's teaching about half the kids, if she's lucky. That response is sloppy—letting the kids lead. OK, c'mon lady, you don't even have one kid reading there. The only one reading is the goddamn teacher."[26]

As a result of such harassment, the Grand Rapids educators insisted that the materials be reviewed by the National Education Association, the Michigan Education Association, and the Michigan Department of Civil Rights. The Council on Interracial Books for Children ran a lead article on the *Distar* program in which Vivian Gamon described the use of *Distar* and its limitations nationally, attacking the method as well as the content:

> *Distar* is by no means a new educational concept, as some believe. Actually it has taken the worst of traditional American teaching methods and refined them. While it purports to teach the basic skills to "disadvantaged" children, a close analysis reveals assumptions and methods which work against the very children it claims to help.
>
> The false assumption that the language of poor children is insufficient for logical thought helps perpetuate the equally false view that such children are somehow inferior. The emphasis on rote memorization and on endless repetition promotes the development of pupils who have no need to think except superficially. The assumption that children will only learn if there are external rewards such as raisins and candy reflects our society's attitude toward work and the alienation people feel from their own work. It also teaches children to work not for their own satisfaction, but for a specific set of external rewards.
>
> Just as *Distar* does not believe that children can learn for their own "internal" satisfaction, so it mistrusts teachers and insists that they not teach unless their every action is strictly prescribed. The teachers' guides tell them when to speak, what to say, when to stop, at what point to praise and the precise words they are to use. Words of praise become a predicted response and lose all sincerity. The pupil–teacher relationship becomes impersonal; teachers and pupils perform like robots—the former act and the latter react obediently and unquestioningly on cue. Any deviation from the boring, repetitious script is considered a waste of time.
>
> And underlying all of this is the racist and classist assumption that minority and working class children need this sterile, one-tracked, rote approach if they are to learn. Ignored is the need for a curriculum that shows respect for different cultures and different languages, that stimulates imagination and creativity and that provides books to inspire interest and excitement in reading."[27]

For the school systems which cannot afford to turn in all the books in the system for new ones, there are procedures that teachers and administrators can use to evaluate books, readers, and tests used in kindergarten through 12th grade.

Detroit, Michigan, public school staff members prepared a set of 12 questions to use in judging the human relations content of books: Does this book:

1. Avoid the use of stereotypes and caricatures in portraying group differences and group characteristics?
2. Appear to be free of unnecessary language or material which would tend to offend any racial, religious, or ethnic group?
3. Clearly indicate through illustrations and/or content the fact that America is a multiracial nation?
4. Give adequate representation to the contributions of the many racial, religious, and ethnic groups which are a part of our society?
5. Indicate that within each group there is a wide range of individual differences?
6. Present the environmental and historical influences which have been instrumental in developing group differences where they exist?
7. Portray each culture, race, and ethnic group in a manner which will develop understanding, acceptance, empathy, and respect?
8. Present the forces and conditions which have worked to the disadvantage of minority groups, so that the student is led to make accurate and unbiased judgments regarding intergroup conflicts?
9. Analyze conflict situations honestly and objectively with emphasis on possible solutions to intergroup tensions?
10. Help children recognize prejudice as something which prevents mutual understanding and appreciation for the rights of others?
11. Provide motivation for children to examine their own attitudes and behavior in relation to their democratic value?
12. Help children develop wholesome democratic values and note their importance to good citizenship and to a happy life?[28]

The U.S. Commission on Civil Rights has prepared a *School Self-Study Guide*.[29] Included in it is a content analysis worksheet to evaluate textbooks about their treatment of minority groups (specifically, the American Indian, the black American, and the Spanish-surnamed American).

The "Green Circle" program is designed to increase awareness of the problems of prejudice and discrimination. Created in 1957, by Gladys Rawlins, under the auspices of the Race Relations Committee of the Philadelphia, Pennsylvania, Yearly Meeting of the Society of Friends, the program is now incorporated and has been implemented in schools in almost all the 50 states. Community groups with an interest in education and human relations have sponsored "Green Circle" programs in elementary schools. If a community has no trained demonstrator, "Green Circle" will arrange for a presentation to help schools determine whether they wish to implement a program. The program depends on volunteers. Training manuals and demonstration kits are available through the central office in Philadelphia.[30]

"Green Circle" is presented through the use of a flannelboard, children participation, and classroom follow-up by the teacher, usually to early elementary school pupils. During the initial presentation, some of the premises of the program are discussed:

- A green felt circle denotes life and growth.
- Our circle of life should be unending; no one should be shut out.
- The circle grows to include family, friends, community, county, state, nation, and world.
- Everyone is equal.
- The green circle is a circle of love.

Following the classroom presentation, it becomes an individual project of the pupils and teacher. Materials are provided for follow-up games and activities, all reinforcing the initial presentation. The major strength of the program, in my opinion, is that it provides a vehicle for teachers to take a positive approach toward race relations and awareness in the early elementary school years.

"Role models" are rarely present for black children in schools. The proportion of certified black teachers and principals is low. Less than 3 percent of the certified reading specialists and reading supervisors in the United States is black. Black children who live in black neighborhoods and attend all or mostly black schools are taught by white teachers (with materials about white middle-class America) and tested with tests designed for and by whites. Fear that racism does exist perhaps explains why reading teachers search far and wide for the causes of reading problems in our urban schools, rather than looking at the school and what goes on in the school behind closed doors.

George Weber, of the Council on Basic Education, completed a very interesting research study to attempt to determine why children read so poorly in inner-city schools.[31] He identified some criteria for inner-city schools—"a nonselective public school in the central part of a large city that is attended by very poor children"—and some criteria for reading success—"achievement of national grade norm or better as a median and an unusually low percentage of nonreaders." Weber eventually identified four inner-city schools that were successful in reading: P.S. 11 in Manhattan, the John H. Finley School (P.S. 129) in Manhattan, the Woodland School in Kansas City, Missouri, and the Ann Street School in Los Angeles. Weber wanted to find out what it was about these four schools that made them more successful in teaching reading than other inner-city schools. What were the variables for success? He assumed that when the successful schools followed a practice not usually found in an unsuccessful school, that practice had something to do with the success. Weber found eight practices in the four schools that were not present in other schools.

1. Strong leadership—the principals really cared. They encouraged high-quality teaching of reading.
2. High expectations—the teachers believed the children could perform better than inner-city kids usually perform.
3. Good atmosphere—although admittedly hard to describe, Weber sensed a relaxed atmosphere and a lack of disorder, noise, and tension.
4. Strong emphasis on reading—reading was the "first among equals" in each school.
5. Additional reading personnel—all four schools had reading specialists in the primary grades.
6. Phonics—all four schools recognized the importance of teaching word-analysis skills.
7. Individualization—there was concern for the progress of each individual child.
8. Careful evaluation of pupil progress—related to No. 7; frequent evaluation of each child was a practice in each successful school.

He further discovered that factors such as small class size, achievement grouping, quality of teaching, ethnic background of principals and teachers, preschool education, and outstanding physical plant were not present in the better schools, although they are factors generally believed to be important.

There are, of course, many other conditions that could be changed to help minority children make greater progress in reading:

• use of more relevant materials
• use of criterion-referenced tests (see Chap. 7)

- acceptance of various language dialects
- better preparation of teachers for inner-city positions
- rejection of the belief that minority children and white children differ in innate abilities

However, these changes will make little impact by themselves. There simply is no substitute for a teacher who believes that each child can learn to read and knows how to teach the necessary skills.

There are some extremely disturbing ideas that have developed from much of the current research on urban education and reading. Study after study focuses on the restricted language of the urban poor, the deprivation of early childhood, and, at the extreme, the supposed lower intelligence of blacks. Many "scholars" have all but concluded that minority children cannot achieve without intervention in their homes and integration with higher-status white children. Some research serves to perpetuate the myth of minority inferiority. The only way one can ever prove inferiority is to have all other variables equal. Simply stated this means: equal teachers, equal facilities, equal living conditions, and an equal past. Those who naively believe that three new reading clinics in a poverty area, or a new "Head Start" program, or a small increase in black personnel, or a brand-new school can even remotely be considered as evidence of equalization are simply unaware of both the daily and long-term impact of racism on black children. Scholars still mention racism in passing as they move on to some "more important" points about abstract reasoning ability or noise level in the ghetto.

Researchers have carefully scrutinized the child and designed and redesigned the methods and materials used in teaching beginning reading. However, they have not called attention to what is truly missing in urban schools: the systematic teaching of reading skills. Few research studies or reports focus on the breakdown of *teaching* in urban schools. In classroom after classroom more attention is devoted to how we can *control* students, especially minority students. Attend any workshop or education conference and the number-one concern of urban teachers is not instruction but discipline. However, casual observation of hundreds of urban classrooms reveals little, if any, systematic *instruction*. There is no basis for concluding that poor and minority children have serious difficulties in learning to read. That conclusion would only be justified if high reading failure was still evident after systematic instruction by sympathetic teachers had taken place.

In their study of racism, Louis Knowles and Kenneth Prewitt sum up the problem this way:

> An individual working alone can do very little about racism in American Institutional life; he will be swallowed up by the

sheer size of the problem. To work for institutional change, it is necessary to develop a rough analysis of the ways local institutions operate and how they contribute to the subordination and exploitation of black people . . . the organization must get down to specific issues as soon as possible. Most American people are tired of sweeping generalities and vague statements. If they are seriously ready to work on racism, then they should be able to dig right into a particular issue that has a bearing on their own lives . . . the task forces should find out who else is already working in the areas of concern and consult them immediately. Very often much time and research effort can be saved by learning from others who have been working on the issue for a longer time.[32]

Censorship

Other children fail at reading for many other reasons discussed in this book, and once they fail at reading they become turned off to *any* book as long as it represents a "reading" task. So the later elementary teachers, junior and senior high school teachers, and some college teachers are faced with the task of turning students on to books. It follows then that the teachers have to find books that are so appealing, so exciting, so in tune with the child's or the adolescent's interests that the motivation to read a particular book will overcome the threat of reading. This is no easy trick, especially when teachers and parents feel the need to *censor.*

The old battle whether "this book" or "that book" should be allowed in the classroom is well known. If we, as adults, are told, "Don't read that book, it's pornographic," we will perhaps read the book to check the evidence for ourselves. We can accept or reject what is presented and make our own decisions and personal judgments. Children are usually not given this freedom. Through readability levels, grade levels, and the moral judgment of a librarian or an editor, books that enter the reading classes are strictly controlled.

Psychologists like Jean Piaget[33] tell us that children can make up their own minds, that they do have critical perceptions. Often, teachers are afraid to have children read what they, the teachers, are afraid to deal with themselves. We must give children the option of choosing a "bad" book. Teachers rarely do, and this perpetuates censorship, which undermines personal choice and learning how to make decisions.

Teachers and authors are not the only censors for young readers. The following excerpt from an article in *The New York Times* describes other attempts to censor reading materials used by young readers.

A survey of the most recent six-months' issues of the American Library Association's Newsletter on Intellectual Freedom, which reports censorship cases of all kinds nationwide, provides a seismograph recording on what the book removers are up to. During this period there were approximately 25 incidents involving complaints about books from public or high school libraries or assigned reading lists. Books attacked included: "Manchild in the Promised Land," "Down These Mean Streets," "I Never Promised You a Rose Garden," "The Me Nobody Knows," "Love Story," "One Flew over the Cuckoo's Nest," "Soul on Ice," "Sylvester and the Magic Pebble," "Catcher in the Rye," "Revolution for the Hell of It," "Do It!," "Woodstock Nation," "Daybreak," "Rabbit Run," "A Farewell to Arms," "Slaughterhouse-Five," "The Grapes of Wrath," and the works of William Faulkner and Hermann Hesse, to name some.

Complainants ranged from individual parents (including two Indian parents who protested against textbooks that portrayed Indians as savages) to organized groups. Among the latter were local parent-teachers associations, the International Conference of Police Associations, the Ridgefield, Conn. Taxpayers League, the Admiral Rickover Parents and Taxpayers Association, various boards of education, police chiefs, the Constitutional Heritage Club, the American Legion, the John Birch Society, Morality in Media, Citizens for Decent Literature, the National Association for the Advancement of Colored People and the Montgomery, Alabama Human Relations Council. (The last two named were opposed to "Little Black Sambo.")

Reasons offered for banning the books most frequently revolved around "filthy language." (Ol' Holden Caulfield has been suffering from that one for a long time.) Black writers such as Eldridge Cleaver, Malcolm X, LeRoi Jones, Claude Brown and James Baldwin were anathematized for bad language but mainly for their radical politics. A Houston school board received complaints that four Am. Lit. textbooks were "heavy on sociopolitical approach emphasizing an anti-military, anti-bomb atmosphere." "Sylvester and the Magic Pebble," a children's book by William Steig that won the Caldecott Award, offended police because the policemen in the book were represented as pigs—pink ones at that. (Sylvester's

parents were donkeys, but no parent complained—*mea culpa?*)
Works by John Updike, John Steinbeck, Ernest Hemingway
and J. D. Salinger were condemned as "pessimistic, morbid
and depressing." "Slaughterhouse-Five" was anti-Christian.
And so it goes.

Now, none of these books could conceivably be found
obscene under Supreme Court guidelines, so it wasn't *really* a
question of protecting minors from pornography. Whatever
the motives, and we are not by any means ascribing evil to
them, the effect was censorship of the ideas expressed in these
books, the author's personal view of the human condition.
Especially vulnerable were books by black writers—an unconscious racism?—and emanations of the counter-culture. (A
bookseller was arrested for selling "Do It!" to a 14-year-old boy;
Joan Baez's "Daybreak" was banned in one school because it
contained a four-letter word, but Miss Baez was identified as a
"radical.")

So if sometimes the complaint is ostensibly four-letter
words, it is becoming increasingly difficult to tell where obscen-
ity leaves off and fear of radical political and cultural ideas
begins. Did the Flushing, Queens, school board ban Piri
Thomas's "Down These Mean Streets" solely because of the
street talk or did some atavistic middle-class fear of the ghetto
creep in?"[34]

In 1974, national attention was focused on the Kanawha County,
West Virginia, schools and a controversy over the use of multicultural
textbooks. Schools were closed and demonstrations took place over the
use of such books as Houghton, Mifflin's *Interaction* series (edited by
James Moffett, 1973). The reading books that were censored were
publishers' attempts to provide exciting, real-life material. To help
resolve the controversy, the Kanawha Community Association of
Classroom Teachers asked the National Education Association (NEA)
to investigate. After 2 days of on-site testimony by 77 witnesses, the
NEA published its report.

> In discussing the significance of the Kanawha County textbook
> controversy for public education and for school systems
> throughout the country, the N.E.A. panel considered two
> specific questions:
>   1. Had it not been for their multicultural, multiethnic
> content, would the language arts materials adopted in 1974
> have generated as unyielding and violent a protest as that
> which has occurred?

2. Would the conflict have been as prolonged and in-
tense as it was, had it not been infiltrated by representatives of
highly sophisticated, well organized right-wing extremist
groups?

The answer to both these questions, the panel believes, is
no.[35]

While the censors are feverishly protecting the morals of young
people, and the young people are reading the books identified to them
by the censors as "must" reading, in back of the proverbial barn or
under the covers with a flashlight, good teachers are still faced with the
dilemma of turning kids back on to reading who have been turned off.
Well, one way to do it, we might as well admit, is with "dirty books."
Why do "dirty books" turn kids on to reading? As stated earlier, kids
are not naturally inclined to read. Especially at the beginning, using the
natural interests of the children is one of the most successful approaches to teaching reading. We all know what children's interests
are. Why do we continue to require books like *Ethan Frome*? It makes
sense, when dealing with older children, who for one reason or another
have been turned off to reading, to help them find books that will
appeal to their natural interests.

It may be hard to believe, but teachers are not always in touch
with the interests of children, or with popular literature. In 1965, I
delivered a keynote address to the faculty of a large school system. I
mentioned my use of Salinger's *Catcher in the Rye* as a book to turn kids
on to reading. After the speech, a teacher approached me and asked,
"Could you tell me the author of the book you mentioned—*Catch Her in
the Rye?*"

In a northeastern city recently, an all-black 9th-grade English
class, all 30 of whom reportedly were tested as reading at the 3rd-grade
level or below, were given two books to read. The books were *Nigger*[36]
and *The Autobiography of Malcolm X.*[37] Both books had been previously
banned from the school. Given books that related to their own
backgrounds and experiences, the 9th graders not only "read" the
books—one way or another—but, in addition, every one in the class
scored better than 70 percent on a comprehension test on the books.
These two books are clearly difficult for students who have reading
problems, but the contents were so powerful for those particular students that they read them. Hopefully, many of the students went on to
overcome their "reading problems." For many of them, one of the two
may have been the first book they ever read, or at any rate the first book
encountered in school which appealed to their natural interests.

In 1966, it was discovered that a Job Corp program was using
"lurid books."

JOB CORPS CENTER USED LURID BOOKS

Kilmer Chief Found Youths
Learned to Read Better

By RONALD SULLIVAN

Special to The New York Times

EDISON, N.J., Sept 5—The director of the disbanded Job Corps Center here said today that the use of thousands of racy, sex exploitation paperbacks had raised the low reading level of young corpsmen.

The use of the cheap paperbacks was discovered when a scavenger in a local garbage dump came across a discarded file folder from the defunct center at Camp Kilmer, which had been the corps' Eastern showcase. The folder contained a 27 page purchase invoice listing dozens of sexually provocative titles sent to the center from a bookstore in New Brunswick.

D. L. Weber, the former Job Corps director, at first refused to acknowledge that the books had been used in the center's remedial reading program. However, reached at the International Telephone & Telegraph Company headquarters in New York City, Mr. Weber ultimately conceded that the center had used the "sexy titles" to persuade the 18- and 19-years old corpsmen to read when they would read nothing else.

Keith Perkins, an I.T.&T. public relations official, also confirmed the purchase of the books but he said the official who bought them had been dismissed.

Spur to Better Reading

Mr. Weber, who ran the Kilmer center as an official of the Federal Electric Corporation, a subsidiary of I.T.&T. under a contract with the Federal Government said: "The paperbacks generally did improve the reading level. It got them to go to better things, such as history and the classics."

However, the publisher of the paperbacks that had the most provocative covers initially had no idea that his line was to be used to raise the reading and cultural level of the 5,500 young men who were trained here for manual and technical employment.

"At first I thought they were kidding," Walter Zacharius, vice-president of Lancer Books, Inc. said in his office in New York City. He recalled that it had "seemed strange" to him that the center had ordered so many of his erotic paperbacks and had ignored his line of "96 teen-age classics. But I guess they wanted to get those boys to read anything, as long as they read," he said.

Popular Titles

Although Federal Electric officials refused to comment, at least $10,000 in sex exploitation paperbacks were purchased in a one-month period last fall. They were ordered from the Rivoli Book Store and the invoice listed such titles as:

"Male Nymphomaniac," "Call House Madam," "The Man From O.R.G.Y.," "The Girl From Pussycat," "Warm Bed in Reno," "Teeny-bopper in the C.I.A." Other selections among the 10,860 paperbacks included the popular "Candy" and "Fanny Hill."

In addition, the Job Corps purchased one paperback atlas and 10 copies of "How to Build a Better Vocabulary" and "Thirty Days to Better English."

Officials at Camp Kilmer, which is now the headquarters for the New Jersey Residential Manpower Center, said none of the paperbacks were there now. The Job Corps Center was disbanded June 30 and the new center, which will be operated by the State Department of Education, will open in October.

The Rivoli Book Store in New Brunswick has gone out of business. The store's former manager, Donald Boyle, said the books he sold to the Job Corps were "no longer my bag." He has since turned his store into a mod shop that features hippie clothes and incense for the undergraduates at Rutgers University.

According to Mr. Weber, the theory behind the purchase of the suggestive titles was in line with the reading program being advocated by Daniel Fader, a member of the English faculty at the University of Michigan. He said the idea was to bombard young people with all kinds of reading in the hope that enough would be absorbed to lead them to higher levels.

Mr. Weber said the paperbacks in question were no worse than a large number of novels that had been accepted by contemporary society.[38]

In is doubtful that the lurid books alone were responsible for raising reading levels. However, teachers need *some* means of opening the door, some means of getting kids to the point where they are ready, willing, and able to profit from instruction in reading. "Dirty books" are one of many possible ways of turning kids on. Good teachers, of course, are the primary means. The saddest commentary, however, is that such tactics have to be used at all—that kids are so turned off that teachers have to use "dirty books" to "bribe" them back to reading.

Sexism

Along with the women's rights movement has come the "discovery" that females are discriminated against in textbooks, school readers, and children's literature. Such organizations as the National Organization for Women, Women on Words and Images in Princeton, N.J., Feminists on Children's Media in New York, and Interracial Books for Children in New York have publicized the sex stereotypes perpetuated in school books. The organizations have lobbied for changes through books, newsletters, and monthly updates. They have successfully pressured publishers to publish writers' guidelines.[39,40] They have encouraged school systems to evaluate books. New books on sexism in education and literature have been published as a result of their efforts. Rarely does a school system adopt a new text or set of readers today without checking the content for various stereotypes. The publishers have responded by indicating their awareness. However, a debate still goes on over how the woman's role is portrayed in classic literature. Should we rewrite the classics? Is it discrimination or healthy propaganda? As Selma Lanes, a critic and reviewer of children's books, puts it:

> The truly memorable books we read as children or as adults usually deal with the triumphs of human beings over one sort of spiritual bondage or another. And while it is certainly true that members of minority groups and women in contemporary society do face special problems, it is also true that long after women have attained their equal rights and today's minorities have achieved full acceptance, the great human problems—failure to communicate with one another, love unrequited or lost, an individual's grasp forever exceeding his possibility for achievement in a single lifetime—will still confront us all, both young and old. And we will continue to look to works of true literary quality and depth to shed light on them. Thus, let's all welcome books of healthy propaganda, but let's recognize them as just that and not make them the mainstay—or the main preoccupation—of our children's reading diets.[41]

There has been such a flurry of activity in the area of identifying sex stereotypes in reading materials that a national resource center on sex roles in education was established in 1973 by the National Foundation for Improvement of Education. They publish an occasional newsletter indicating the latest developments in the movements. The center's address is Suite 918, 1156 15th Street, N.W., Washington, D.C., 20005.

Women on Words and Images in Princeton, N.J. (P.O. Box 2163, Princeton, N.J., 08540), has published two books which are representative of the literature on sex bias. They are *Dick and Jane as Victims,* a study of 134 school readers from 14 publishers in which boy-centered stories outnumber girl-centered stories 5 to 2, and *Channeling Children,* an analysis of sex stereotyping on prime-time television.

It is well known that reading problems occur among boys five times as frequently as they do among girls. This ratio continues among juvenile offenders, school dropouts, and adult criminals. There is a strong relationship between reading problems and all of the above populations. It doesn't seem too farfetched to draw a relationship between reading problems and sex stereotyping in school books. At least the speculation is interesting. The majority of elementary school teachers are female and have been for some time. Assuming that many female schoolteachers have been brainwashed by the sex stereotyping—girls are gentle, the weaker sex; boys are stronger and boisterous; and reading is a gentle, female activity—then it follows that the teachers would unconsciously have higher expectations for girls' reading ability than for boys'. Furthermore, given the assumption that our entire society has been subtly "had" by the material we read as we grew up, then it is not surprising when we hear of the father, on seeing his son reading a book, asking, "Why aren't you out playing baseball like a normal 10-year-old boy?" Research studies of sex differences in reading have studied teacher influences, hereditary causes, challenging books, girls' earlier physical maturation, and girls' earlier achievement in certain reading areas.[42] The studies have *not* conclusively laid the blame with any one variable. It is likely that the cause is cumulative, all of the above factors contributing to boys' reading problems. I would suggest that the variable of sex stereotyping of books may just be the most pervasive of the many causes. After all, can't we blame the majority of teachers being women on the role stereotyping in literature over the years?

There is no doubt that racism, censorship, and sexism have all played a negative part in reading instruction and will continue to do so until the concern and awareness of parents and the general public eliminates them.

References

1. Shaner, Madeleine, *Halls of Anger,* Paperback Library, New York, 1970, pp. 49–52.
2. Gallo, Donald, *Recipes, Wrappers, Reasoning and Rate,* a Digest of the First Reading Assessment, National Assessment of Educational Progress, U.S. Government Printing Office, Washington, D.C., Report 12-R-30, April 1974, p. 39.

3. *Ibid.*, p. 56.
4. Kerner, Otto, et al., *Report of the National Advisory Commission on Civil Disorders*, E.P. Dutton, Inc., New York, 1968.
5. Clark, Kenneth, "Answer for the Disadvantaged is Effective Teaching," Annual Educational Review, *The New York Times*, January 17, 1970, p. 50.
6. Woodworth, William, and Salzer, Richard, "Black Children's Speech and Teacher's Evaluations," in *Urban Education*, vol. 6, Sage Publications, Inc., Beverly Hills, Calif., 1971, p. 171.
7. Williams, Frederick, "Language, Attitude, and Social Change," in *Language and Poverty*, Markham Publishing Co., Chicago, 1970, pp. 388–389.
8. Rist, Ray, "Student Social Class and Teacher Expectations: The Self-fulfilling Prophecy in Ghetto Education," *Harvard Educational Review*, vol. 40, No. 3, 1971, pp. 70–110.
9. Leacock, Eleanor, *Teaching and Learning in City Schools*, Basic Books, Inc., New York, 1969, p. 205.
10. U.S. Commission on Civil Rights, *Teachers and Students*, Report V, Mexican-American Education Study, U.S. Government Printing Office, Washington, D.C., March 1973.
11. Amidon, Edmund, and Flanders, Ned A., *The Role of the Teacher in the Classroom: A Manual for Understanding and Improving Teacher's Classroom Behavior*, Paul S. Amidon Associates, Minneapolis, 1963, pp. 6–11.
12. U.S. Commission on Civil Rights, *op. cit.*, p. 21.
13. *Ibid.*, pp. 22–23.
14. *Ibid.*, p. 33.
15. *Ibid.*, p. 27.
16. *Ibid.*, p. 39.
17. *Ibid.*, p. 40.
18. Torrey, Jan, "Illiteracy in the Ghetto," *Harvard Educational Review*, vol. 40, May 1970, p. 253.
19. Corwin, Ronald G., *A Sociology of Education, Emerging Patterns of Class, Status, and Power in the Public School*, Appleton-Century-Crofts, New York, 1965, pp. 83–84.
20. Dunn, Lloyd, *Peabody Picture Vocabulary Test*, American Guidance Service, Inc., Circle Pines, Minn., 1959, plate 76.
21. Dunn, Lloyd, University of Hawaii, personal correspondence, 1971.
22. Yackel, John P., President, American Guidance Service, Inc., personal correspondence, 1971.
23. Dove, Adrian, "The Dove Counterbalance Intelligence Test," copyright 1968 by Dove/Jet, reprinted by permission of Adrian Dove. A complete copy of this test can be found in Daigon, Arthur, and Dempsey, Richard A. (editors), *School: Pass at Your Own Risk*, Prentice-Hall, Inc., Englewood Cliffs, N.J., 1974, pp. 146–149.

24. Chall, Jeanne, *Learning to Read: The Great Debate,* McGraw-Hill Book Co., New York, 1967, p. 292.
25. Englemann, Siegfried, and Stearns, Susan, *Distar Learning to Read,* several levels, Science Research Associates, Inc., Chicago, 1972.
26. Divoky, Diane, "Education's Hardnosed Rebel: Ziggy Englemann," *Learning,* vol. 1, January 1973, pp. 29–31, 68.
27. Gamon, Vivian C., "Bias Pervades *Distar* Content," *Interracial Books for Children,* vol. 5, December 1974, p. 1.
28. From *Detroit Schools,* published by the Detroit Board of Education, October 29, 1968, by permission of the Detroit Public Schools.
29. U.S. Commission on Civil Rights, *School Self-Study Guide,* U.S. Government Printing Office, Washington, D.C., 1973.
30. The Green Circle Program, Inc., 112 South 16th St., Philadelphia, Pa., 19102 [Telephone: (215) LO-3-3666].
31. Weber, George, *Inner-City Children Can Be Taught to Read: Four Successful Schools,* Council on Basic Education, Washington, D.C., October 1971.
32. Knowles, Louis L., and Prewitt, Kenneth (editors), *Institutional Racism in America,* Prentice-Hall, Inc., Englewood Cliffs, N.J., 1969, Epilogue.
33. Piaget, Jean, *Science of Education and Psychology of the Child,* Orion Press, Willows, Calif., 1970 (see the stage of concrete operations in thinking).
34. Lingerman, Richard, "The Last Word: Freedom to Read," *The New York Times,* Book Review Section, October 31, 1971, © 1971 by The New York Times Company, reprinted by permission.
35. National Education Association, Teacher Rights Division, *A Textbook Study in Cultural Conflict,* N.E.A., Washington, D.C., 1975.
36. Gregory, Dick, *Nigger,* E.P. Dutton, Inc., New York, 1964.
37. Malcolm X, and Haley, Alex, *Autobiography of Malcolm X,* Grove Press, New York, 1966.
38. Sullivan, Ronald, "Job Corps Center Used Lurid Books," *The New York Times,* September 5, 1966, © 1966 by The New York Times Company, reprinted by permission.
39. *Guidelines for Equal Treatment of the Sexes,* McGraw-Hill Book Co., New York, 1975.
40. *Guidelines for Improving the Image of Women in Textbooks,* Scott, Foresman & Co., Chicago, 1974.
41. Lanes, Selma, "On Feminism and Children's Books," *School Library Journal,* January 1974, pp. 23, 26–27.
42. Betts, Emmett, *Foundations of Reading Instruction,* American Book Co., New York, 1957, pp. 29, 137.

SEVEN

TESTING AND READING

In 1971, the superintendent of a small-town school system invited me to evaluate the high school reading program. I agreed to spend a day talking to the teachers, visiting classes, and talking to the students. Two days before my visit, I received in the mail test scores of 7th through 12th graders on the Iowa Silent Reading Test sent to me by the high school guidance counselor. At that time The Iowa Silent Reading Test, was known to be one of the worst reading tests available (it was completely rewritten in 1973). The 1965 *Sixth Mental Measurement Yearbook,* one of seven yearbooks containing critical reviews of such tests, warned,[1] "The Iowa Silent Reading Tests should not be used unless they are thoroughly revised . . . this reviewer is of the opinion that the Iowa Silent Reading Tests, in their present form, no longer serve the purpose for which they were intended."

When I visited the school, I met with the guidance counselor first. "Have you ever heard of the *Mental Measurement Yearbooks?*" I asked. "Sure, there they are on my shelf," he answered. I pulled down the sixth and showed him the above review. "Well, how about that," he said. "We've always used that test, ever since I've been here." He was over 60. I didn't ask him how long he'd been there.

Since World War I, the testing movement in the United States has grown with the demand for evaluation. Particularly after the expansion of legislation providing more and more money for education during the 1960s, Congress began asking, "What are we getting for our money? Are kids learning more as a result of all the money poured into education?" At the same time, the need for individualization was being recognized. The realization that children from different ethnic groups, different cultures, and different social classes needed to be treated differently by schools was slowly emerging. It was inevitable that the philosophy of changing the kids to meet the needs of the schools, represented by the federal legislation poverty programs with

their accompanying tests for evaluation, and the philosophy of changing schools to meet the needs of kids, represented by civil rights
workers, educational iconoclasts, and minority groups, would eventually clash head on.

As state and federal education programs demanded more and
more that kids be tested, that programs be scrupulously evaluated (by
testing kids even more), that teachers be held accountable (by also
testing the achievement of kids), and that more and more program
objectives be written which required evaluation, the measuring instruments were bound to come into question. Kids began to be labeled
as underachievers or as mental defectives because they knew a different language or culture than that of the test content. Teachers began to
spend more than 3 weeks in a 6-week summer program testing kids.
Programs began to get sterile, mechanical, and inhumane. And, in the
late 1960s, the humanists stepped in with a barrage of literature bitterly
attacking schools. (Perhaps the best known was Silberman's *Crisis in the
Classroom*. He emphasized the adjective "joyless" in characterizing
schools.) These authors represented the thousands of parents,
teachers, and kids who were fed up with changing kids to meet the
needs of the schools. They demanded a critical look at schools,
teachers, and the use of tests. As a result many large school systems,
including New York City, gave up the use of tests altogether. To this
day many schools simply do not measure IQ.

Anyone who has attended school in the past 40 years is familiar
with school testing programs and has taken a standardized test. They
have heard the words:

> "Don't turn the page until I give the signal."
> "Stop, put your pencils down."
> "Make a heavy black mark."
> "You read the directions silently while I read them aloud."

What are these tests all about? Over 902 tests have been published for the purpose of measuring reading, although only a few of
these are widely used. According to Marjorie Kirkland of Troy State
University, based on an exhaustive review of the literature on tests,
during the 1960s three to five standardized tests were given to each
elementary and secondary school child each year.[2] I would guess that at
least one of those was a reading test or a group of tests including one on
reading. There are seven categories of reading tests and a discussion of
each follows.

Reading achievement tests. These tests are the most widely used.
There are specific reading achievement tests and also lengthier
achievement tests called batteries (which also test arithmetic, science,
and other areas). A score on a reading achievement test purports to tell

how much a child has learned in reading. Scores on these tests are usually recorded as grade-level scores, by grade and month (4-3 equals 4th-grade, 3rd-month reading level). Some scores are reported in percentiles. If a child's score is at the 70th percentile, she did equal to or better than 70 percent of all the children who have taken the test. Standardized tests are usually given to a large number of children all over the country prior to their publication, so the publishers' "norms" (average or normal scores) will be representative of children all over the country. The tests are called "standardized" because scores of a large number of children are available for comparison purposes.

Oral diagnostic tests. These tests indicate the kinds of mistakes a child makes when reading aloud. The mistakes are labeled as omissions, substitutions, mispronunciations, and the like. The assumption is that oral reading is not different from silent reading. But we know that when a child reads orally, all kinds of pressures (an adult is present, the child knows a test is being given, the child fears making a mistake, etc.) are placed on the child. Scores on these tests are also recorded as reading grade levels, but their stated purpose is more to determine specifically the *kinds* of errors a child makes when reading aloud. What they really test most effectively is anxiety while reading aloud.

Silent diagnostic tests. These tests, in a series of subtests which measure various areas of basic reading and comprehension skills, report a reading grade level for each skill tested. Usually tested are such "comprehension" skills as directed reading, sentence meaning, poetry comprehension, vocabulary, paragraph meaning, location of information, and the like. Even if we knew what these skills were, research on reading comprehension has clearly shown that it is impossible to separate them adequately on a test to measure them in isolation.[3] Understanding what one reads is a very complicated process that depends on the reader's knowledge and experience, purpose, intelligence, frame of mind, attitude, and many other factors. Educators have pretended that they can measure how a reader interprets a piece of literature and measure whether the reader is correct or not correct. They have stretched this foolishness by saying that thinking ability can be measured in isolated little parts. It simply cannot be done.

Readiness tests. These tests usually include several auditory and visual discrimination (hearing and seeing likenesses and differences) tasks to determine whether preschool, kindergarten, and 1st-grade children are ready for formal instruction. If the child can do "reading-like" activities, then he or she is ready. I prefer to attempt to teach the child to read to determine if the child is ready, willing, and able to profit from instruction.

Speed reading tests. These tests measure the number of words one can read per minute. They also provide questions at the end of reading to check comprehension or how much one remembered and interpreted from the reading selection. Many high school and college reading comprehension/achievement tests record a reading rate, but the reading rate score is not a speed reading score. Good speed readers adjust their rate of reading to their purpose, the difficulty of the material for them, and their attitude of the moment.

Perceptual tests. These preschool tests are used to determine learning disabilities and cognitive, or mental, abilities. They have gained popularity as the idea of identifying learning disabilities has become popular. Children are usually asked to do tasks like tracing and drawing figures. These will be discussed in the chapter on remedial reading and later in this chapter under learning disabilities.

Intelligence tests. These tests fall into two categories: group and individual. They are supposed to indicate a child's "mental age." This is translated into an IQ, or intelligence quotient, by comparing the mental age with the child's actual age. The differences between the group and individual tests are important in reading, because the group tests, which can be given to a large group of children at one time, require reading ability to complete. Reading teachers often use the difference between mental ability and reading ability to indicate how many grade levels a reader is behind. If a child has a problem reading and scores poorly on a group intelligence test because of it, he either appears to have no problem or he may be placed in a special class because of his seemingly low mental ability. For many years, children who achieved at a higher level than their score on an intelligence test would predict were called "overachievers." Today we know how inaccurate the tests can be.

Individual intelligence tests (the most well known are the *Wechsler Intelligence Scale for Children*[4] and *For Adults*[5] and the *Stanford-Binet Intelligence Scale*[6]) are sold only to psychologists and require special training to administer. Because of this, these tests are not widely used in school reading programs, even though they are the only halfway valid individual tests available.

All of these tests have been attacked vehemently in both the popular press and professional literature. Debby Meier, coordinator for open education in District 2, New York City, has written a position paper outlining the biases of reading tests.[7] Her list of seven biases neatly summarizes the literature on reading test bias in the late 1960s and early 1970s.

1. *The Language Dialect of the Test: Standard English.* Such tests are, by their very nature, biased in favor of children whose home

and neighborhood use Standard English, and who are thus familiar and comfortable with this particular pronunciation, vocabulary, and syntax.

2. *Middle-Class Bias of Tests.* They are biased in favor of children who have had a specific type of middle-class experience with life—in terms of vocabulary, style of speech, knowledge of life, associations, and values.

3. *Bias of Tests Toward Conformity and Stereotype Thinking.* They are biased in favor of children with fairly conventional, conforming, and uncreative thinking patterns—even within that middle-class culture.

4. *Bias of Tests Toward Early Reading.* They are biased in favor of children who mature early in terms of verbal skill, and thus penalize later maturers.

5. *Speed Bias of the Tests.* They are biased in favor of those who think and work quickly, thus penalizing children whose thinking and working processes are more cautious or careful.

6. *Emotional Bias of the Testing Situation.* They are biased in favor of children who are emotionally and socially secure under competitive and judgmental pressures.

7. *Teaching Strategy and Learning Theory Bias of Tests.* They are biased in favor of children who have been subjected to certain methods of teaching reading and certain related theories about learning to read. They thus penalize children who are learning in different ways. As a result, they tend to confirm their own biases and to lock schools into specific teaching strategies that are increasingly under question by linguists, learning theorists, teachers, and parents.[8]

One of the most damaging results of the use of tests is that reading test scores set up expectations in the minds of teachers. The self-fulfilling prophecy works deviously enough by labeling children "remedial readers," but it is even worse when a child is said to have a "learning disability." Reading specialists and others use tests to label children. "Learning disability" is the label of the 1970s. Diane Divoky showed great courage in writing "Education's Latest Victim: The 'LD' Kid":[9]

> In the 1950s, the schools discovered psychology, and the reason for kids not making it became "emotional handicaps." In the 1960s, the emphasis was sociological; failures were "culturally deprived" or "disadvantaged." Each set of labels shared with the others a common characteristic: it specifically put the blame on the child himself, his family, the society, or the school.[10]

A veritable institution has grown around this new "illness." Divoky highlighted the new tests accompanying the "learning disability" movement:

> The battery of tests goes on: VMI, Frostig, Peabody, ITPA, WISC, House-Tree-Person, WRAT, Bender, Hooper, Visual Acuity, perceptual motor, visual motor, audition. Tests to uncover dyslexia, dyscalulia, aphasia, agnosia, distractibility, mixed dominance, dyspractic movements, developmental lag, CNS damage, minimal brian dysfunction, or other new names indicating a variation from the magic norm of the diagnostician.[11]

Divoky's article will be dismissed by many as the naive work of a layperson, but she asked important questions and revealed questionable practices used in schools for the past 10 years.

Despite enormous evidence against the use of standardized tests in schools, they continue to be used. In one survey of 714 elementary school principals across the country, only one principal reported that the school did not give standardized tests.[12]

Even reading specialists themselves have attacked norm-referenced tests on the grounds that they lack a theoretical base. Kenneth Goodman, a reading professor at Arizona State University, said:

> Essentially, a test is no better than the theory of the reading process on which it is built. Unfortunately, reading tests, like most tests, are not built on an articulated theoretical base. Rather, they are built up of bits and pieces, skills, elements or essentials loosely organized around a view often not stated, of what reading is. Without theory, tradition plays a vital role— new tests measure what old tests did, and tests grow by adding new parts to old aggregates. The theory of testing, complete with statistics, is likely to be more sophisticated than the theory of reading in any given reading test.
>
> If a test were based on a stated theory of reading, it could be criticized on the basis of the validity of its theoretical base and its consistency with that theory. In the absence of such a base, reviewers must react to the bits and pieces or confine themselves to evaluating the statistical support.
>
> The latter often takes on the form of an elaborate scaffolding supported by skyhooks. National grade norms or percentiles are carefully established for tests that may be quite inappropriate in some areas and ethnic populations. Separate scoring for diagnostic sub-tests are developed when, in fact, the

sub-tests correlate so highly in given populations that they appear to be testing the same thing.

More basically, none of the scores or grade norms of percentiles provide any useful information about what a pupil should know or be able to do at any stage in developing reading proficiency.[13]

At the same time that reading tests are being attacked so bitterly both within and outside the reading profession, it is incredible that the USOE just completed a several thousand dollar project which perpetuates the use of the tests being criticized. They chose eight popular standardized reading tests and made it possible to compare a score on one of them to a score on all the others as follows:

> This study presents an approach to equating scores from widely known reading achievement tests given to children in grades 4, 5, and 6 and aims primarily to provide a means for wide distribution and use of the Anchor Test Study raw-score equivalences, individual norms, and school-mean norms. The tables in this manual, compiled from data collected on these tests, are intended to facilitate conversion of a score on one of the eight tests to an equivalent score on any one of the other seven. In addition to providing procedures for using the data, the manual contains brief analyses and a summary of the study design.[14]

Intelligence tests are just as bad. These tests have been widely criticized by a variety of authors, particularly since the article by Arthur Jensen appeared in the *Harvard Educational Review* in 1969.[15] Jensen's racist claim that blacks have inferior intelligence caused a reevaluation of intelligence testing. Two excellent studies which discuss the misconceptions and fallacies of intelligence testing are *The I.Q. Cult* by Evelyn Sharp (Coward, McCann and Geoghegan, New York, 1972) and *The Fallacy of I.Q.* (Okpaku Publishing Co., Inc., New York, 1973) edited by Carl Senns. Jerome Kagan, professor of developmental psychology at Harvard University, offered a clear statement of the problem in 1971:[16]

> The concept of intelligence is among the most confused ideas in our lexicon, for ambiguity surrounds its definition, etiology, and social significance. A central issue turns on the degree to which scores on standard intelligence tests reflect generalized quality of memory and reasoning that is not limited to a particular cultural setting. It is our view that the relation between a person's score on a contemporary I.Q. test and his ability to think logically and coherently is poor. Moreover, the psycho-

logical trait "intelligence," which unfortunately has become equated with the I.Q. score, has become a primary explanation for the unequal access to power in our society.

Criticisms of reading tests have also appeared in the prestigious *Mental Measurement Yearbooks* (edited by Oscar K. Buros, Gryphon Press, Highland Park, N.J.) for years. These yearbooks, published periodically since 1938, contain critical reviews of all educational and psychological tests written by acknowledged experts in the various fields. In 1968, the first yearbook was published which dealt only with reading, *Reading Tests and Reviews,* a compilation of all prior reviews of reading tests into one book; in 1975, *Reading Tests and Reviews II* was published, containing reviews of more recent reading tests.

Some excerpts from critical reviews of well-known reading tests follow. (The excerpts have been lifted out of context. I would recommend reading the entire reviews of specific tests for complete information. The *Mental Measurement Yearbooks* are usually available in administrative offices in school systems.)

About a new test:[17]

> While the test's ideas and format appear to be promising, at the present time the *Carver-Darby Chunked Reading Test* is clearly not ready for general use. The test purports to be both a valid measure of information stored during reading, and "an indicator of individual differences in reading comprehension." These claims have not been substantiated by the manual. The reliability and validity studies reported can be best described as pilot studies from which the test appears to have some promise.

A review of a test which claims to be a revision of a popular, older test.[18]

> The set of skills and strategies that make for success in taking this test may have no direct relationship to those called into use by a successful reader. The component which the authors state is the most significant—comprehension—is the least touched. If comprehension can be understood to involve judging a reader's ability to interrelate information and draw conclusions, while avoiding the use of background and simple recall information, it would seem necessary to use much longer and more fully developed reading selections.

From a review of a diagnostic reading test:[19]

> Validity studies have not as yet justified the division of comprehension into discreet sub-skills. Because a lack of knowledge exists about basic aspects of comprehension, real doubt is

cast on the validity of subtests that purportedly measure specific components of comprehension. *The Diagnostic Reading Test* is no exception to this validity problem.

About a checklist to determine if a child has dyslexia:[20]

In summary, the reviewer sees no possible reason for the use of the *Dyslexia Schedule.*

About a prereading screening test for learning disabilities:[21]

Most of the subtests assess more than one characteristic, making judgment regarding the various abilities difficult and subjective. The scoring is highly subjective and not necessarily based on the variable under consideration.

Concerning an $1,890 eye-movement camera:[22]

The *Reading Eye II* is a well-designed and easily-operated instrument which yields little useful information not obtainable from paper-and-pencil tests or mere observations. Its one striking asset is that students are fascinated with the camera and the aura of science that it generates. For those reading specialists who believe that this factor is worth the price, the *Reading Eye II* would be an excellent choice.

About a popular oral reading test:[23]

The *Gilmore Oral Reading Test* requires individual administration, and is rather time consuming, and the results have limited use in view of the invalid assumptions upon which the test is based. It would therefore seem that the time might be much better spent on a well-constructed informal reading inventory which tests oral reading with an oral test and reading comprehension with a silent test, and which samples types of comprehension, not simply recall of details.

And, lastly, a test of "perception":[24]

In summary, the *Developmental Test of Visual Perception* does not appear to be able to assess specific areas of perception differentially. Its global perceptual scores, particularly the P.Q., have reasonable reliability and predictive powers. Users are cautioned against assuming that low scores on the *Developmental Tests of Visual Perception* are a signal to begin perceptual training.

Publishers are particularly vulnerable to criticisms of tests. The publisher's interest is simply economic. Dr. James Carmody, a measurement specialist, observed:[25]

It might be argued that test-producing companies have a vested interest in maintaining a certain level of ignorance about the use and validity of their tests. Certainly, if their efforts to inform people about how their tests should *not* be used were as vigorous as their selling campaigns, which emphasize the tests' potential uses, the present knowledge gulf between test builder, seller, and user would not exist. It is very difficult to imagine a testing company representative requiring a potential user to pass a test purporting to measure his competence in using a certain test and its results before selling him the test. Since, in actively informing educators of the limitations of their tests, testing companies run the risk of substantially reducing sales, it is very difficult for them to be totally responsible.

The only solution to the problem of standardized reading tests is to junk them all—they are not useful. Roger Farr of Indiana University, one of the most respected measurement experts in reading and a member of the board of directors of the International Reading Association, summed up his feelings on reading tests very neatly in 1971.[26]

The following questions about reading comprehension tests were raised in 1910; were reiterated in 1938; and are still being asked today:

1. Why is there such a great overlap between measures of hypothesized different skills of reading comprehension?
2. What format should reading comprehension measures take: Multiple choice questions? Cloze? Fill in? Long passages or short? Should examinees be allowed to look back at a selection when answering questions?
3. What are the subskills of reading comprehension?
4. How strong an effect does prior knowledge of a topic have on an examinee's reading comprehension?
5. Does the language structure of a selection affect reading comprehension?

I suggest that these and other similar questions result in exercises in futility. The only validity of any importance is how well a test predicts a student's ability to perform functional reading tasks. *Reading measures need to be developed which are based on specific reading tasks and purposes for reading* (italics mine).

Just as we have been generally disillusioned with our attempts to measure intelligence as a psychological construct, perhaps we should be disillusioned with our attempts to measure reading comprehension as a psychological construct. The measurement of reading comprehension should be based on an attempt to determine how well a reader can accomplish a given task with a given reading selection. From my perspective, the history of the measurement of reading comprehension got started on a narrow, single track over fifty years ago and has been chugging around in circles ever since. That is not to say that increased sophistication in the technical, scientific, and even artistic aspects have been non-existent. Indeed, some of the advances in those aspects have been quite dramatic, but the essential problem is that the train has never switched off the initial track, it has just had a streamlined engine attached.

What Farr was asking for was criterion-referenced testing rather than norm-referenced testing. Standardized tests are norm-referenced tests, tests which can be given to children to compare them to an established norm (normal score for an average child in his or her age or grade range). The score one gets on a norm-referenced test is a grade-level score or a percentile score, both of which are meaningless as far as telling us what a child knows or doesn't know. Criterion-referenced tests tell us what skills a child knows or has and does not know or have, information that can be used to improve the teaching–learning situation with that particular child. A reading grade level of 4.5 or a percentile score of 50 is meaningless. However, if we have a list of basic word-analysis skills that a child does not have, then we know what to teach her. A norm-referenced test supplies a 1.5 grade-level score on word-analysis skills for a child with normal intelligence in the 3rd grade. Teachers interpret that to mean that the child needs help with word-attack skills. A criterion-referenced test given to the same child might say that she knows the beginning consonant sounds b, m, c, and so on, but that she cannot read words with double vowels when the first vowel has the long sound, like bead, read and raid.

Farr called for a change to criterion-referenced testing both in the article quoted above and in his book, *Reading: What Can Be Measured?*[27] He also criticized several reading tests for not measuring what they claim to measure. Along with the usual rewards attending the successful publication of a book came offers from two test publishers: he became the author of new versions of the *Iowa Silent Reading Test*[28] and *The Metropolitan Achievement Test.*[29] Both were norm-referenced tests and had been severely criticized.[30,31] The new tests are still norm-referenced Why? Because the sales force said, "How are we going to sell a test without grade equivalents?" said Farr.[32] School systems want to compare one school with another, and they want to see growth in grade levels from year to year. He says now that "there is no such thing as a non-criterion referenced test."[33] In my opinion, Farr fell into the trap that many reading professors have fallen into. Even though he admitted he doesn't believe in grade equivalents, he authored a test with grade equivalents. For the purpose of profits for the publishing companies and perhaps for furthering their own careers, authors perpetuate these tests, knowing that they perpetuate labeling, tracking, and poor teaching. But authors are the first to excuse themselves by saying, "It's not the tests that are bad, it's the people who use them," the same arguments that are used to defend alcoholic beverages, guns, and automobiles, three of our society's deadliest weapons.

Criterion-referenced tests probably never will become widely used, even though such tests are clearly better than norm-referenced tests, as indicated by the research activity in the measurement field on criterion-referenced testing.[34] Dr. Ronald Hambleton, a measurement specialist at the University of Massachusetts, has indicated the major threat of criterion-referenced testing:

> . . . Criterion-referenced tests can be used to evaluate the effectiveness of instruction. Norm-referenced tests given at the end of a course are usually inappropriate in evaluating the effectiveness of instruction because they are not designed to cover the instructional objectives. However, criterion-referenced tests are useful in this regard because the test can be constructed so that the results will specifically measure the instructional objectives.[35]

The tests, used widely, would provide a valid tool for evaluating teachers. We could evaluate children's reading skills based on the teacher's stated objectives. Norm-referenced tests will not do this.

Research and Testing

If measurement specialists continue to test out the feasibility of criterion-referenced tests and they do become widely used, an added benefit will be the improvement of research on the teaching of reading. Unfortunately, practically all research studies in reading are based on norm-referenced tests because it is so easy to compare one group of children with another using these tests. Reading research is analogous to the story of the proud Texan:

> . . . And the Texan, who claimed he was the best six-gun shot in the West, would take those who challenged him to the side of an immense barn and fire aimlessly. He would find where his bullets had landed and then draw targets with his bullet in the

bull's eye every time! Moral: He aimed at nothing so he couldn't miss!

There has been more research and fewer tangible results in the area of reading than in any other area of education, usually based on testing kids. Research on reading has been shoddy, ill-designed, irrelevant, misconceived, and generally a waste of time and money. It was this lack of good hard data on the reading process that caused the federal government to step in with specific programs like Title I and Title III of the 1964 ESEA Act. Even though funding for many promising government programs has been cut off, over 15 million dollars was spent in the late 1960s and early 1970s on reading research. Samuel Weintraub of the State University of New York at Buffalo, one of the leading experts in the reading research area, outlined in a book for teachers[36] what research has discovered about learning to read. He acknowledged that, "Compared with accomplishments in most other sciences, reading research is still in its infancy."[37] He summarized for teachers why reading is taught the way it is. Here are some of the conclusions he reached, based on research evidence:

Reading readiness. Many factors interweave that permit a child to learn to read.

Language development. Oral and written language are closely related. Oral language of young children is relatively sophisticated. The development of concepts in young children is closely related to the growth in their vocabulary. When concepts have been clarified, a child's performance tends to be more accurate.

Auditory discrimination. Being able to hear likenesses and differences in sounds is one of the factors essential for success in learning to read.

Visual discrimination. Being able to see likenesses and differences in letters is a factor basic to success in learning to read.

Primary reading. The influence of the teacher appears to be important here. Approaches to reading may vary depending on the effectiveness of the teacher. Certain methods may be better for some children than for others.

Word recognition cues. Children use syntactic and semantic cues in reading. In other words, children learn words better in context than in isolation.

If this is the best advice we can give teachers after years and millions of dollars of testing and research, then a great deal of time and money are being wasted on research on the reading process. The above conclusions are just plain common sense. Reading research is based on the ideas that the complicated interactions between teachers and children, and between children and materials/techniques, make the differences in learning to read. We should leave the research on *learning* to the psychologists and concentrate on the *facilitation* of learning by encouraging good teaching. The country's illiteracy rate is evidence enough of poor teaching of reading in our schools. More research and testing results aren't going to help teachers with the kids who have learned to hate reading and kids who have not learned to read.

We need data on teaching. Are good teachers born, not trained? Are open attitudes and knowledge of subject matter basic to good teaching? Is actually teaching in a classroom the only way to learn teaching? Does learning take place solely by facilitation by the teacher and discovery by the child? How do teachers facilitate intrinsic motivation? How do we measure affective, or emotional, factors in reading? What are the different aptitudes children have for reading? How do we measure them? What kinds of instruction match what kinds of aptitudes in learning to read? These are some of the questions we should be asking in reading research, instead of continually inventing new ways to test, label, and blame children for their illiteracy.

I am by no means the first to criticize reading research, as the following examples show.

William S. Gray, 1950:[38]

> Unfortunately, much of the scientific work relating to reading has been fragmentary in character. As pointed out by various writers, the investigator frequently attacks an isolated problem, completes his study of it, and suggests that he will continue his research at some later time, but often fails to do so. In the second place, there is far too little coordination of effort among research workers in the field of reading. . . . In the third place, many of the studies reported have been conducted without adequate controls.

C. Winfield Scott, 1954:[39]

> Of the various weaknesses of reading research, these three seem most important. Inadequate controls, poor control groups, and weak criteria of success. . . .
>
> The most tantalizing and stimulating characteristic of reading research findings is their inconclusiveness. In reviewing a recent summary of studies on mixed eye-hand dominance, Gray concluded, "Obviously final conclusions relating to this problem cannot be stated at present." This statement could be written large after every area of reading research.

The situation is desirable in a number of respects, but to the extent that it arises from faulty or uncoordinated research, it is inexcusable.

Charles C. Fries, 1963:[40]

. . . the very mass of the materials creates great difficulty. But the difficulties do not arise out of the volume of the materials alone. One comes away from a concentrated study of hundreds out of the thousands of these investigations much distressed. He seeks in vain for the cumulative continuity that has characterized all recognized sound scientific research. He struggles hard, without success, to find the strands of fundamental assumptions and accepted criteria of sound procedure running through a series of studies attacking any of the major problems of the teaching of reading.

George D. Spache, 1972:[41]

A reading researcher retires to his study to dream up a new technique in reading instruction. After two or three days, he emerges to try out his idea on a few children in some cooperative school; the results are inconclusive. He reports his findings at the next national convention and presto! he has created a new way of teaching reading. He may have some doubts about his gimmick, but the teachers and publishers who implore him to share his brainstorm with them obviously do not.

In the *Second Handbook on Research on Teaching,*[42] a project of The American Educational Research Association, there is a large section called "Research on Teaching of School Subjects." Ten different school subjects are covered. Reading is not one of them.

One of the major breakthroughs in the battle against bad tests recently came from an unlikely source—the U.S. Congress. President Ford signed into law on August 21, 1974, a bill that allows parents and students to see school and college records.[43] The "Buckley Amendment" (to a lesser known library bill) allows parents the right to look at their children's cumulative files, the records passed on from teacher to teacher as children go through school. Often these records contain opinions of teachers based on test scores. These opinions often set up expectations in the minds of the teachers who read them. The children, of course, behave the way they are expected to behave when so treated. The Buckley Amendment will remove much damaging material on kids before parents ever see the cumulative records, and if there are any remaining damaging comments, the parents who look will find them.

References

1. Buros, Oscar K. (editor), *Sixth Mental Measurement Yearbook,* Gryphon Press, Highland Park, N.J., 1965, p. 795.
2. Kirkland, Marjorie C., "The Effects of Tests on Students and Schools," *Review of Educational Research,* vol. 41, October 1971, p. 303.
3. Davis, Frederick B., "Research in Comprehension in Reading," *Reading Research Quarterly,* vol. 3, Summer 1968, pp. 499–545.
4. Wechsler, David, *Wechsler Intelligence Scale for Children,* The Psychological Corporation, New York, 1949.
5. Wechsler, David, *Wechsler Adult Intelligence Scale,* The Psychological Corporation, New York, 1955.
6. Terman, Lewis M., and Merrill, Maud A., *Stanford-Binet Intelligence Scale,* Houghton, Mifflin Co., Boston, 1960.
7. Meier, Deborah, "Reading Failure and the Tests," an occasional paper of the Workshop Center for Open Education, New York, February 1973.
8. *Ibid.,* pp. 5–6.
9. Divoky, Diane, "Education's Latest Victim: The 'LD' Kid," *Learning Magazine,* vol. 2, October 1974, pp. 20–25.
10. *Ibid.,* pp. 23–24.
11. *Ibid.,* p. 20.
12. Goslin, D. A., Epstein, R. R., and Hallock, B. A., *The Use of Standardized Tests in Elementary Schools,* Technical Report No. 2, Russell Sage Foundation, New York, 1965.
13. Goodman, Kenneth S., Review of *Reading Tests and Reviews* (Buros, Oscar K., Gryphon Press, 1968) *American Educational Research Journal,* January 1971, pp. 170–71.
14. Department of HEW, *Anchor Test Study,* USOE publication S/N 1780-01312, 1974, 92 pp.
15. Jensen, Arthur, "How Much Can We Boost I.Q. and Scholastic Achievement?" *Harvard Educational Review,* vol. 39, Winter 1969, pp. 1–23.
16. Kagan Jerome, "I.Q.: Fair Science for Dark Deeds," *Radcliffe Quarterly,* March 1972, pp. 3–5.
17. Gullickson, Arlen R. (reviewer), *The Carver-Darby Chunked Reading Test,* review in *Seventh Mental Measurement Yearbook,* vol. 2, edited by Oscar K. Buros, Gryphon Press, Highland Park, N.J., 1972, p. 1072.
18. Burke, Carolyn L. (reviewer), *Gates-MacGinitie Reading Tests, op. cit.,* p. 1080.
19. Plessas, Gus P. (reviewer), *Diagnostic Reading Test: Pupil Progress Series, op. cit.,* p. 1115.
20. Kling, Martin (reviewer), *Dyslexia Schedule, op. cit.,* p. 1137.

21. Jamison, Colleen B. (reviewer), *Pre-Reading Screening Procedures, op. cit.,* p. 1141.
22. Geyer, John J. (reviewer), *Reading Eye II, op. cit.,* pp. 1144–1145.
23. Smith, Kenneth J. (reviewer), *Gilmore Oral Reading Test, op. cit.,* p. 1148.
24. Mann, Lester (reviewer), *Marianne Frostig Developmental Test of Visual Perception,* 3rd edition, *op. cit.,* p. 1276.
25. Carmody, James, "Some Controversial Issues in Testing," in *Controversies in Education,* edited by Dwight W. Allen and Jeffrey Hecht, W.B. Saunders Co., Philadelphia, 1974, p. 364.
26. Farr, Roger, "Measuring Reading Comprehension," in *Reading: The Right to Participate,* Twentieth Yearbook of the National Reading Conference, edited by Frank P. Greene, NRC, Inc., Milwaukee, 1971, p. 196.
27. Farr, Roger, *Reading: What Can Be Measured,* International Reading Association, Newark, Del., 1969.
28. Greene, H.A., Jorgensen, A.N., and Kelley, V.H., *Iowa Silent Reading Tests,* Harcourt, Brace and World, New York, original copyright 1927, since revised.
29. Allen, Richard D., et al., *Metropolitan Achievement Tests,* World Book Co., New York, original copyright 1934, since revised.
30. Jones, Worth R. (reviewer), *Iowa Silent Reading Tests: New Edition,* review in *Sixth Mental Measurement Yearbook,* edited by Oscar K. Buros, Gryphon Press, Highland Park, N.J., 1965, p. 1070.
31. Wilson, Susan, and Moulton, Elizabeth, "The Unfair Tests," *The New York Times,* September 18, 1971, p. 29.
32. Farr, Roger, speech at Grand Rapids, Mich., October 17, 1974.
33. *Ibid.*
34. Hambleton, Ronald K., "Assessing Student Progress: A Criterion-Referenced Measurement Approach," in *Controversies in Education,* edited by Dwight Allen and Jeffrey Hecht, W. B. Saunders Co., Philadelphia, 1974, p. 375.
35. *Ibid.,* p. 372.
36. Weintraub, Samuel, "What Research Says About Learning to Read," in *Coordinating Reading Instruction,* edited by Helen Robinson, Scott, Foresman & Co., Glenview, Ill., 1971, pp. 180–201.
37. *Ibid.,* p. 180.
38. Gray, William S., "Reading," in *Encyclopedia of Educational Research,* edited by Walter Scott Monroe, Macmillan Co., New York, 1950, p. 966.
39. Scott, C. Winfield, "A 'Forest' View of Present Research in Reading," *Educational and Psychological Measurement,* vol. 14, Spring 1954, pp. 208–214.
40. Fries, Charles C., "Past Practice and Theory," in *Linguistics and Reading,* Holt, Rinehart and Winston, Inc., New York, 1963, p. 3.

41. Spache, George D., *The Teaching of Reading,* Phi Delta Kappa Foundation, Bloomington, Ind., 1972, p. 149.
42. Travers, Robert M. W. (editor), *Second Handbook of Research on Teaching,* Rand McNally and Co., Chicago, 1973.
43. *The Family Educational Rights and Privacy Act of 1974,* Public Law 93-380, vol. 23, No. 32, August 21, 1974.

EIGHT

REMEDIAL READING

The statement that schools do more harm to kids under the guise of remedial-reading instruction than in any other area is shocking but true.

Until that statement can be said to be false, I, as a reading specialist, find it very hard to exert much of my energy or interest in the area of reading disabilities or remedial reading. We know very little about how a child learns to read. We know even less about why children do not learn to read. Nearly every course and book on the topic of teaching reading has a section on the reading process. These courses and books explain, some in very intricate detail, what the reading process is all about—in the opinion of that particular author or instructor. There are as many explanations and definitions of what happens when one reads as there are reading specialists. To define the reading process completely would necessitate defining all the intricate relationships among the psychological, physiological, biological, affective, linguistic, cognitive, neurological, psychomotor, and hundreds of other factors that influence learning and reading. One would also need to determine whether reading to learn can be separated from learning to read. To define the reading process would be to answer most of the questions psychologists and educationists have been asking for years about what goes on behind the eyes.

Only in the late 1960s did reading specialists realize that they did not have a definition of reading or a description of what reading is. They began to ask themselves what reading is, mostly in response to government contractors who, in 1967, began making money available for basic research on the reading process in order to define reading. To date, they do not appear to be any farther along in defining reading than they were when they started.

Remedial reading deals with children who do not learn to read in regular classrooms and who are disabled in other areas because they cannot read. Usually these children cannot be identified until they are in the 5th or 6th grade. Some children are called remedial cases if they exhibit one of the hundreds of indicators even before they go to school. We know so little about reading and identifying problems, and yet everyone has an answer. Remedial reading has become a very lucrative field. Parents of children with reading problems go from expert to expert, spending and spending until they find the "expert" who has the answer for their child. Psychiatrists, psychologists, optometrists, medical doctors, and teachers (good and bad) have all gotten into the act. All one need do is hang out a shingle saying that he or she has an answer to reading problems, and the clients will parade to the door, money in hand.

The International Reading Association has no standard licensing procedures whatsoever for reading specialists. Half the states do have licensing procedures, but they are based on courses rather than competence. Parents are usually not informed of their child's reading problems until the schools realize that they are helpless to treat them. The schools do not have competent reading specialists to take over problems caused by incompetent teachers. Parents typically raise hell with the school for a while but eventually turn to the yellow pages or to one of the many organizations that have sprung up to meet the needs of parents of children who have reading disabilities, like The Orton Society, state and national associations for children with learning disabilities, university reading clinics, hospital pediatric clinics dealing with reading, or to people in the community who have a reputation for dealing with reading problems (usually outside of the schools), perhaps a psychologist, a former teacher, or an optometrist. All of these "experts" claim to have a record of success.

Three major ideas have led us to the situation we are in now regarding reading disabilities: 1) children have reading problems; 2) remedial reading works; 3) if a child can't read, she has a learning disability.

Children Have Reading Problems

The idea is stated in many ways in this book that schools and teachers, not children, have reading problems. Schools have a "blame-the-victim"[1] problem. The literature on reading outlines in detail the reasons children do not learn to read. If all those words, books, articles, and reports were devoted to ways in which children *do* learn to read, they might enable schools to help children learn to read. As it is, teachers are very reluctant to blame reading problems on themselves. Rather, they blame them on genetic factors, perceptual difficulties, developmental lag, hyperactivity, lack of physiological integration, disadvantaged background, emotional maladjustment, ego deficiencies, a variety of other factors related to the child—and instructional methods or techniques. All of the above causes of reading problems are related to the child (except the last one). They have been studied in depth. Remedial techniques are available. These include everything from "creeping and crawling" to "patterning" (moving the head and arms in a rhythmic pattern) to prescribing drugs. Teachers and schools let themselves off the hook. Descriptions of children with reading problems are typically prefaced by such statements as, "Despite X years of conventional teaching, Mary continues to. . . ." Or, "After 4 years of school, Jerry still does not read." Augmenting the problem, many teachers' expectations of children, particularly black and minority students, are so low that they unconsciously or consciously neglect to teach them. The statement made by so many reading teachers that, "Frank is reading very well though he comes from *this area* or *that neighborhood* or *that family* . . .," automatically labels the teacher as one who discriminates in teaching. Teachers who make such statements have negative expectations for children, and the children usually fulfill these expectations.

Remedial Reading Works

That remedial-reading classes, "perceptual" classes, and "learning-disability" classes, or whatever such classes are called, are successful is a myth that has been debunked for years, yet remedial-reading teachers continue to be hired and remedial-reading programs continue to be designed. Typically, teachers develop a bag of tricks, games, and gadgets which are intended to capture the imagination of children. The teachers see thousands of gimmicky items in packages and boxes of "programmed excitement" peddled by the publishers. These remedial tricks are used in the name of motivation. "The child must be motivated to really want to read," says the remedial-reading teacher.

The fact is that most kids who are poor readers have been conditioned to hate reading from the 1st grade on. They have been conditioned to believe that learning to read is not fun. Then the remedial-reading teachers step in with their fun and games. The fun and games do turn the kids on. They want to play. But it is the fun and games that excite the children, not reading, which, in fact, is difficult. The idea that remedial tricks work is ridiculous. They are like a turn-of-the-century quack doctor's patent medicines. School systems are buying huge quantities of these cure-alls in the forms of reading machines and boxed programs every day, which work no more successfully than the quack's patent medicines. Some publishers have developed teaching programs to test for reading problems, and then learning programs to help kids do better on the test, which is a small-scale monopoly in itself. None of the activities has anything to do with reading.[2]

Actually, remedial-reading programs are the schools' "holding operation." Remedial-reading programs, once established in elementary schools, high schools, and colleges, are thought to indicate that the school is "doing something" about reading problems. But the research evidence is that remedial-reading programs don't work. Bruce Balow, a professor at the University of Minnesota, argues in an article on using "perceptual-motor" activities in the treatment of reading disabilities:

> Since research on motor and perceptual programs for children with severe reading disability offers little support for the easy answers promulgated these days, a conclusion that perceptual-motor activities are desirable may be surprising. Although there is no body of experimental evidence supporting a direct effect of perceptual-motor activity on basic skills, and it is clear that such activities are neither "cure-alls" for the general run of learning disabled pupils nor specific to any basic school skill, the case studies reported in the literature argue for the possibility that visual-motor programs may be a specific treatment for a few very unusual children. That, however, even if it were to be found true, is insufficient reason to argue the desirability of perceptual-motor activities for all pupils.[3]

James C. Reed, of Tufts University School of Medicine, concluded as a result of a large-scale study of tests used to diagnose reading disability:[4]

> Teachers and reading specialists should view with considerable skepticism any statement pertaining to the so-called intellectual, cognitive, or perceptual deficiencies of retarded readers. Many of the statements are interesting speculations, but nothing more. The particular pattern of deficits may represent only an artifact of the investigator's decision to use one measure of potential instead of another. A child's potential for reading is probably much more closely related to the materials and methods used for teaching than some arbitrary index of expectancy.

Alan Cohen, formerly of Yeshiva University, now a reading consultant for Random House, in a published debate over the efficacy of remedial-reading programs,[5] stated: "To put it succinctly, on the basis of present data, I would play the visual perceptual game if I were in the visual perception or the IQ business. But in the reading field, the surest way to get urban kids to read is to teach them letters and words and to do it thoroughly."

Norman and Margaret Silberberg reported that:

> Research in remedial reading which utilized control groups consistently has demonstrated two outcomes:
>
> 1. Tested reading achievement is significantly higher in the group which received remediation than in the control group at the completion of the remedial period.
>
> 2. Follow up studies almost invariably demonstrate that the beneficial effect of this remediation "washes out" in a relatively short time after terminating remedial reading.[6]

Yet, in the face of all the evidence that most remedial programs don't work, we continue to support them while ignoring what should be the real concern—teachers and schools.

If a Child Can't Read, a Learning Disability Is Present

This myth could have different titles, like: *Reversing* d *and* b *Means You Can't Read, Reading* saw *as* was *Spells Disaster in Reading,* or *Serious Association Problems Can Easily Be Cured if You Use the Right Method,* and so on.

Serious reading difficulties are very lucrative for the people who claim to have the answers. For other reading professionals, serious reading difficulties present a never-ending source of concern and frustration. Serious reading difficulties, learning disabilities, dyslexia, or whatever one chooses to call serious reading problems, may affect as much as 2 percent of the total school population.

Since there is no licensing procedure in the reading field other than in the few states that have state certification for public school reading teachers, anyone who is hired as a reading specialist becomes the diagnostician. Serious medical problems are referred from licensed physicians to licensed specialists for particular illnesses. In schools, the classroom teacher, having taken one reading course, might become the reading specialist who recommends what the teacher learned from that class, what the teacher read in *McCall's,* or (and this has actually happened) what the teacher read in a drug-company advertisement. The *McCall's* article stated:

> At least one child in seven has a serious learning problem, a disability that torments him now and will plague him all his life.

Most schools seem unable to deal with these problems—or even recognize that they exist—but they can be corrected.

At first you hardly notice. Your child is a bright and happy kindergartner, a little giddy with energy, perhaps, but eager to learn. In his haste he sometimes says "pease" for "please" and "pasghetti" for "spaghetti", but his teacher assures you that many children his age make the same sort of mistakes.

The first-grade teacher introduces her class to the alphabet, and your son seems to master all the sounds. But when he tries to write simple words, "cat" becomes "tac" and even his own name comes out a jumble of reversed letters. Still, his teacher is not alarmed, so why should you be? After all, your son has taken an IQ test that shows his intelligence to be well above average.[7]

Some so-called remedial-reading children exhibit what is called hyperkinesis or hyperactivity: the kids are "fidgety" and they can't sit still. Physicians have discovered that Ritalin® (methylphenidate hydrochloride), a drug which is normally a stimulant in adults, paradoxically acts as a depressant in children. Ritalin is often prescribed by physicians and recommended by teachers for "fidgety" children who also have reading problems. Given the widespread use of Ritalin, Stanley Robin and James Bosco, professors at Western Michigan University, asked 150 elementary teachers in Grand Rapids, Mich., their opinion of Ritalin. Eighty-five percent knew what it was and 95 percent reported they could recognize an overactive child. More than 65 percent had had children in their classes who took Ritalin.[8] Yet, it is reported that it is extremely difficult for practicing physicians (pediatricians) to effectively diagnose hyperactivity or hyperkinesis. James Bosco referred to a study by Kenny and others in the *Journal of Pediatrics*,[9] indicating that 58 percent of children referred to physicians for treatment as hyperactive may not be. Bosco said:

> Since hyperkinesis is not easy to diagnose we were disconcerted to learn that 96% of the teachers in one of our studies felt that they could identify hyperkinetics in their classroom. I believe teachers are overly confident about their abilities to identify hyperkinetic children in their classrooms. More pre-service and in-service instruction for teachers on pathological and normal behavior is needed.[10]

A little bit of knowledge is a dangerous thing, and nowhere are those words as true as they are among teachers. The use of Ritalin is controversial enough, but not as controversial as the definition of "dyslexia." Dyslexia is a word used interchangeably with alexia, word-

"Boy, that Johnny's a real dummy."

That's what the kids say about John because he can't do second grade reading.

His teacher says he's inattentive — won't sit still and try

His mother says he's just a "late bloomer."

And John? He doesn't know what to say. But he himself is beginning to believe that he must be pretty dumb.

The truth is that John has a hidden handicap that makes reading and writing very difficult for him. His brain does not perceive and interpret correctly what his eyes see. The letter b becomes d. The word saw becomes was. He writes the number 3 as ε.

John is just one of an estimated 15 per cent (about 5 in every classroom) of school-age children with a functional learning disability. These children have disorders which may manifest themselves in imperfect abilities to listen, think, speak, read, write, spell, or perform mathematical calculations.

The causes are varied, but the result is often the same. Normal learning becomes a severe strain. The child develops a pattern of failure, becomes inattentive and overactive. Eventually he "turns off" from school and may later become a dropout.

How can these children be helped?

Early and accurate diagnosis is the first step. If you believe your child suffers from some learning disability, talk it over with your family doctor or pediatrician. He may refer you to a psychologist, neurologist, or other physician specializing in sight, hearing, and motor skill problems. Accurate records of how your child has developed from birth can be enormously helpful in pinpointing learning problems.

When a learning disability is recognized, a child can be taught to overcome his handicap with the combined help of doctors, teachers, and remedial specialists.

As part of your family's health care team, we at A. H. Robins recognize the importance of research to make medical techniques more effective in treating learning disabilities. So that more and more Johnnies can have the learning skills necessary for their complete development.

A. H. ROBINS COMPANY, RICHMOND, VIRGINIA
Making today's medicines with integrity...seeking tomorrow's with persistence.

Reproduced by permission of A.H. Robins Company, Richmond, Virginia.

blindness, specific dyslexia, perceptual handicap, minimal brain damage, and, more recently, learning disability, learning disorder, and cerebral dysfunction. The words carry as one of their many meanings the inability to read. Because there is so much controversy over the use and definition of the words, they have all been used to define a syndrome which may include three or four of the following symptoms:

- high intelligence
- overactivity
- poor visual discrimination
- poor auditory discrimination
- poor auditory memory
- poor motor coordination
- brain injury
- lack of reading skills
- inability to creep and crawl
- mixed-hand dominance
- word and letter reversals

There are as many different treatments as there are words to label the problem. It has been my experience that reading specialists who have had training under a proponent of one of the many theories of diagnosis and treatment tend to find what they look for. For example, in 1970, in Omaha, Neb., several physicians were prone to prescribing Ritalin. Sure enough, teachers diagnosed hundreds of children as hyperactive. The use of the drug was so widespread that it caught the attention of the "Huntley-Brinkley Report" on NBC on July 4, 1970. Virginia Brown and Morton Botel provided the best definition I know of this complex area in *Dyslexia: Definition or Treatment?*, a government publication.[11] Another publication which is unique in its objectivity on the topic is the report of the National Advisory committee on Dyslexia and Related Disorders mentioned in Chap. 3.[12] I strongly urge any reader who is interested in this topic to read the two documents. They are both short and quite readable. They report all the facets of serious reading problems, from the various diagnostic procedures to the various remedial procedures in an objective, scholarly fashion. They do not provide ready answers or panaceas, but they do state clearly the problems and what is known about solutions.

The anxiety which exists among parents of children with serious reading problems has spawned thousands of expensive private reading schools and reading clinics. It has even been responsible for state laws which reimburse schools for the salaries of learning-disability teachers (Massachusetts, Michigan, and others). In those states, in order to get state money to pay a reading teacher's salary, the school must identify children with learning disabilities. Just when most states are abolishing the special-education classrooms which labeled children and probably caused mental retardation by isolating borderline cases, some states are now developing new monsters in the forms of "learning-disability" rooms. In the past, special-education classrooms became the dumping ground for the "undesirables"—discipline problems and black and other minority children. If the learning-disability classroom fad continues, schools will have replaced the "special-ed" room with the "LD" room. Jeanne Chall has indicated that in Massachusetts 18 credit hours of college courses are required for certification of a "reading specialist," but only three credits are required of "learning-disability" teachers.[13] If a parent takes a child with a reading problem to the learning-disability teacher, problems will arise. Chall says, "Since in the last analysis it is the child with special needs who suffers if those with the best training do not work with him, it would seem that school systems, and particular schools, need to clarify the roles of these two types of specialists."[14]

An informed public can change this trend. Read the two recommended documents. Please understand, I do not deny that there are children with serious learning difficulties (probably 2 percent of the population), but it appears that teachers are identifying practically every reading problem that appears in their class as a learning disability and a remedial case, kids who should have special help—outside of the teacher's classroom. At the other, less scholarly, end of the spectrum is another book which is appropriate to mention, *The Myth of the Hyperactive Child and Other Means of Child Control*,[15] by Peter Schrag and Diane Divoky, attacks the whole "Ritalin, smart pill, therapy, labeling" scene in education with a vengeance.

I have implied that if teachers and schools did the job of teaching reading successfully the first time around, we would have no need for remedial programs in every school and private remedial programs in virtually every large city in the country.

I don't have any panacea for doing it "right" the first time around, but I do have a suggestion.

The one area of reading instruction which has been ignored for years has been the "affective domain"—attitudes, feelings, emotions, interests, likes, dislikes, values, etc.—those psychological variables which so affect learning. Learning takes place more rapidly and more thoroughly in a positive affective environment than in a neutral or negative one. Positive human relations between teacher and pupil, positive self-concept, self-confidence, and positive relations with other pupils enhance learning. Variables in the affective domain cannot be quantified and measured as easily as areas in the "cognitive domain," that is, those areas of hard learning, memory, reasoning, and other mental processes. Also, many teachers are just plain afraid to involve themselves in human relationships with pupils. Therefore, the importance of the affective domain in learning to read has been virtually ignored.

In perusing recently published textbooks on reading instruction, one would be fortunate to find one book which dealt in any significant way with making reading easier by considering the affective domain. Many reading theorists vocally admit that the affective domain influences learning to read, but there is a paucity of written material on the subject. It is rather obvious that the word has not funneled down to thousands of classrooms across the country.

Barnes Boffey of the Upper Valley Teacher Training Center in Hanover, N.H., stated:

> There is less research and literature on *how* affective factors influence reading and learning than on the fact that they *do* influence these two areas. In looking through the literature, one finds that one author speaks of "attitude toward learning," while others speak of "motivation." Other terms which are used are "affective climate and learning, self-confidence, coping behavior, accurate perception of reality, connectedness, identity, power, trust, industry, and identity."
>
> . . . We must realize that when we speak of affective factors in reading, we are also speaking of affective factors in living.
>
> . . . Learning to read falls within the larger framework of learning and is therefore influenced by the affective stages which influence all learning.[16]

David Krathwahl and Benjamin Bloom[17] have provided a list of stages within the affective domain which influence learning—and therefore reading. My feeling is that at least 60 percent of the variance in learning to read is due to affective rather than to cognitive variables, that is, more failures are due to affective factors than to cognitive factors.

Although learning to read is not a simple act, teachers lead us to believe that it is a fantastically complicated process that only they can handle. We already have enough knowledge about what happens when a child learns to read to be successful in teaching children to read. All the research on the basic reading process, all the models, and all the theories are wheel-spinning evasions of the real issue. About 2 percent of school children have basic learning difficulties which make it extremely difficult for them to learn to read; the other 98 percent can learn to read, given the appropriate teaching, but, given our present rate of illiteracy, it's obvious that the job is not being done.

References

1. Ryan, William, *Blaming the Victim,* Random House, New York, 1971.
2. The efficacy of such programs as the Frostig Program (Frostig, Marianne, and Horne, David, *The Frostig Program for the Development of Visual Perception: Teacher's Guide,* Follett Publishing Co., Chicago, 1964) has been questioned by many authors. Robinson, Helen M., *Perceptual Training—Does It Result in Reading Improvement?,* mimeograph, paper delivered to the International Reading Association Convention, April 1971. This paper contains citations of more than 25 research studies on the relation between visual perceptual training and reading achievement, indicating little if any relationship.
3. Balow, Bruce, "Perceptual-Motor Activities in the Treatment of Severe Reading Disability," *The Reading Teacher,* vol. 24, March 1971, p. 523.
4. Reed, James C., "The Deficits of Retarded Readers—Fact or Artifact?", *The Reading Teacher,* vol. 23, January 1970, p. 352.
5. Cohen, S. Alan, "Studies in Visual Perception and Reading in Disadvantaged Children," *Journal of Learning Disabilities,* vol. 2, October 1969, p. 503.
6. Silberberg, Norman, and Silberberg, Margaret, "Myths in Remedial Education," *Journal of Learning Disabilities,* vol. 2, April 1969, pp. 209–217.
7. Woodward, Kenneth L., "When Your Child Can't Read," *McCall's,* February 1973, p. 48.
8. Robin, Stanley S., and Bosco, James J., "Ritalin for School Children: The Teachers' Perspective," *The Journal of School Health,* vol. 43, 1973, pp. 624–628.
9. Kenny, T., Clemmens, R., Hudson, B., Lents, G., Cicci, R., and Nair, P., "Characteristics of Children Referred Because of Hyperactivity," *Journal of Pediatrics,* vol. 79, No. 4, 1971, pp. 618–623.
10. Bosco, James, *Implications of the Use of Stimulant Drugs for Educational Practices and Policies,* paper presented at the annual meeting of the National School Boards Association, Houston, Texas, April 7, 1974 (available from the author at Western Michigan University).
11. Brown, Virginia, and Botel, Morton, *Dyslexia: Definition or Treatment?* ERIC/CRIER Reading Review Series, 1972, pp. 66–67.
12. HEW National Advisory Committee on Dyslexia and Related Disorders, *Reading Disorders in the United States,* Developmental Learning Materials, Chicago, 1969, pp. 26–28.
13. Chall, Jeanne, "The Special Needs Child: Who Does the Diagnosis and Treatment of His Reading Problems?," in *Proceedings of the Administrators Conference, The New England Consortium for the Right to Read,* October 30–31, 1974; Chicopee, Mass., February 1975.

14. *Ibid.*, p. 16.
15. Schrag, Peter, and Divoky, Diane, *The Myth of the Hyperactive Child and Other Means of Child Control*, Pantheon Books, New York, 1975.
16. Boffey, Barnes, "Affect and Reading: Theory and Practice," unpublished doctoral dissertation, University of Massachusetts, May 1972, pp. 23–25.
17. Krathwahl, David, Bloom, Benjamin, and Masia B., *Taxonomy of Educational Objectives, Handbook II: Affective Domain*, David McKay Co., New York, 1964.

NINE

SPEED READING

In Chap. 4 on publishing, I mentioned that the speed-reading racket is so pervasive in schools, colleges, and business that "speed-reading" information is the only contact the general public may have with the reading field. Indeed, a mother recently told me that her husband had completed a speed-reading course and was training her 2nd-grade son to speed-read. She couldn't understand why the child was having so many problems!

Speed-reading merchants hustle the areas where excellent reading counts—high schools, colleges, and businesses. "Double or triple your reading speed," they advertise, "and increase your comprehension. You won't survive in college or life if you don't read well." It is a known fact that the faster one reads after 200 words per minute, the less one comprehends. Of course, the difficulty level of the material, the prior knowledge of the reader, and the reader's purpose all affect how fast one reads and how much one will understand or comprehend. The average reading speed of college graduates is around 250 words per minute, which is fairly slow. If a person reads 100 words per minute, he would be reading one word at a time and would most likely have difficulty weaving the words together into ideas and concepts. If that slow reader doubled his reading speed, he indeed would increase his comprehension; he'd be reading ideas instead of isolated words.

We know very little about the process of learning to read, but speed reading can be described best by the relationship between what happens in front of the eye and what happens behind the eye. Frank Smith does this in his excellent book, *Comprehension and Learning.*[1] We know that when we read, the eyes make a series of stops called fixations; as they stop, they see about two words, then they jump to the next fixation. Smith describes a classic experiment in perception[2] that indicates the relationship between what happens in front of the eye and

behind it. You can do the experiment yourself by printing three lines on three separate 3 × 5 cards. On the first card write:

CBYAFCBLNGPRVTXC

On the second card write:

AND   WAS   BUT   RED   SEE

On the third card write:

I LIKE TO SPEED READ

Now try the experiment with a friend. Cover the letters with another card and expose (flash) the letters for just a fraction of a second. You'll have to practice this. First show the letters, then the isolated words, then the sentence. Here is what should happen. On the first card, your friend will see two or three letters in the middle. On the second card your friend will see about two words. On the third card your friend will probably read all the words. All three cards presented about the same amount of visual information (in front of the eye). Respectively, the cards had 16, 15, and 16 letters on them. Your friend saw about five times as much on the third card as he did on the first, and he saw two or

three times as much on the second card. The point is that as soon as meaning was added to the letters, your friend started using his prior knowledge about letters and how they go together to make words, and he could see more in one or two fixations as meaning was added to the visual presentation. There is more to reading than just training the eyes to move faster across the page. Without comprehension, there is no reading. If the speed-reading merchants defined reading as comprehension, and actually attempted to teach speed comprehension, then their false claims would not be so dramatic.

At this point, I would like you to complete a little experiment. Please read the following story and answer the question at the end of it.

Reading and Living[3]

It is within the range of possibility that your fortune, and very likely your life, sometime or other, might depend on your ability to read rapidly and with understanding.

You and another officer are in the Navy's intelligence service on a secret mission aboard a large sailing schooner. You are to be dropped off shore about a mile. You are to swim to a prearranged spot on the enemy's shore for a meeting with the chief of the underground. After making contact, you will set up a powerful transmitter to send, in code, information supplied by the underground. You must not fail. The allied forces need this information for an all-out assault on the enemy's mainland.

Success depends on secrecy. You have been secluded in the bottom of a neutral merchant vessel. You reflect that the bottom of a ship is a dangerous place, especially when running a blockade of enemy submarines and fast surface ships.

You and your partner, covered with canvas, lie quietly on the planks of the ship's bottom. Quickly Jim presses his ear against the planks and rapidly whispers, "I hear it, it's a teredo, it's coming this way."

Question

In this situation, which of the following actions would you take?

    a. Run quickly toward the life boats.
    b. Run on deck, prepared to leap overboard.
    c. Sound the alarm, then run to the lifeboats.
    d. Do nothing about it.

Now that you have selected an answer, read on.

Dr. Walter, Pauk, a professor at Cornell University and a respected reading-study skills specialist, wrote "Reading and Living" to shock his students into an awareness of the importance of vocabulary knowledge in reading. No matter how fast you read or how well you read, if you don't know the word meanings, you'll be in trouble. Of course "d" (do nothing about it) is the correct answer. There might be some question about whether Jim can actually hear the teredo (a shipworm, which eats wood) gnawing its way through the planks, but the point is that many people choose to jump overboard, sound the alarm, etc., all for a little worm. The story is excellently contrived to make one think of the danger of a torpedo, but the word is teredo. Comprehension is the goal of reading and the speed-reading merchants prey on that.

The speed-reading merchants place ads in the newspapers, mail advertising, and visit schools and colleges with package deals charging $100 to $200 per student for a short on-campus course plus some follow-up home-study materials. Just recently, a speed-reading program manager attempted to rent a meeting room at my college for 4 weeks without even having the courtesy to ask the college officials for permission to offer a course.

Not long ago a student who was taking teacher-certification courses at our college came to my office and in the course of conversation mentioned that he was teaching a commercial speed-reading course. I had never met anyone who actually taught in one of these programs, although they have been in existence since the early 1960s. I had heard of reading professors attending speed-reading demonstrations and challenging their validity, and I knew some people who had taken a course and shown me their notes. I even got into a letters-to-the-editor battle with the Evelyn Wood Reading Dynamics people several years ago. Here was my chance to talk to a live teacher in such a program. I asked him if he would be willing to have an interview with me and my tape recorder. He agreed and on November 24, 1976, we had the following conversation:

Yarington: How did you hear about the U.S. Reading Lab, or is it the Great Lakes Reading Lab, here in Grand Rapids?

Student: Yes, Great Lakes Reading Lab is a regional office that covers Michigan, Indiana, and, I suppose, Illinois, Ohio, and Wisconsin.

Y: Let me interject something that I'd like to say at the beginning of this interview. You and I have met once before, right?

S: Yes.

Y: In no way did I set you up for this interview. I did not know you ahead of time, and I didn't suggest you be the teacher in the class. This is the first time we've ever talked about speed reading. I just want to make it clear that I have not set you up to do all this so that I could have this interview with you. Yesterday was the first time that we talked about the interview, right?

S: That's correct. I am not an infiltrator into the U.S. Reading Lab, acting on your behalf.

Y: How did you hear about it?

S: I heard about it when I responded to an ad in the local paper for an instructor to teach in speed-reading programs.

Y: Then you responded to an ad in the paper?

S: Yes, the ad that you showed me here.*

TEACHERS

THE NEW ENGLAND READING LAB, "The Speed Reading Specialist," has part-time evening teaching positions available in Oneonta. $8 per hour to start. Small classes, no homework, definitely not sales, but position does require a strong personality with the ability to motivate students and portray competence and confidence. M.A. degree preferred, background in psychology, English, drama or communications considered first. For complete details, send brief vitae, photo and telephone number to: Box XS, c/o The Daily Star. Please do not respond to this ad unless you are willing to work three to five evenings per week (three hours), and can handle the job without constant home office supervision. Position must be filled as soon as possible.

Y: Did you call someone or send a resume?

S: Yes, I sent an application and a cover letter stating what I thought might be sufficient qualifications for the job. It did not, however, include any experience in teaching, but certain experience in education, communications, and psychology. After I sent that in—my resume and

---

*The U.S. Reading Lab, operating out of Texas, has regional offices, one of which is the Great Lakes Regional Lab mentioned above; another is the New England Reading Lab mentioned in the Oneonta (N.Y.) *Daily Star* ad, headed TEACHERS, that appeared on the last day of the special orientation lectures in Oneonta. In other words, "teachers" for the course are advertised for after people have signed up. The ads for students and for teachers are essentially the same in any area where the courses are offered. The student being interviewed had answered an ad in the Grand Rapids paper similar to the one shown from the Oneonta paper.

cover letter—I didn't hear from them for 3 or 4 weeks, and then one day they called and asked me if I wanted to come for an interview.

Y: What kinds of questions did they ask you in the interview?

S: During the interview there was one question that would pertain to qualifications about the job. It was about what background I had in psychology.

Y: They didn't ask you about having had a course in reading or anything like that?

S: I don't recall. They might have, but it doesn't stand out in my mind.

Y: Have you had a course in the teaching of reading?

S: No, I have not.

Y: Have you ever had a course in the teaching of speed reading?

S: In a manner of speaking, yes. The interview that I went to was an all-day affair. I went through the teaching of the entire program, page by page in a manual for teachers which is provided paragraph by paragraph. Afterwards I sat in on the teaching of one of the lessons.

Y: So that interview was also a training session for you?

S: It was. It was much more of a training session than an interview, and I had the impression throughout that they had already decided they would hire me.

Y: But you've never had one of these speed-reading courses or anything like that prior to the day you had the interview?

S: I've never taught one. I took speed reading when I was a kid, probably about 10 years ago, but that was it.

Y: So you had that 1-day session as a training session by the U.S. Reading Lab people?

S: Yes.

Y: Did you have any other training before you started teaching for them?

S: No.

Y: How much does the program cost if I were to come and take your course?

S: If you were a student, it would cost you $179.50, if you could pay that in advance. If you could not, and paid it off in installments, it would cost you $199.50. If you were an adult, out of school, the cost would be $199.50 if you paid it in one lump sum. If you paid it in installments, it would be $219.50.

Y: In the ad, I think it says you can make $8 an hour teaching.

S: That's the initial salary that you receive.

Y: Do they give you raises if you're good?

S: Yes, I now make $10 an hour.

Y: How long are the classes?

S: The class meetings are 3 hours in length. The instructional phase is four class meetings.

Y: How many students are in your classes?

S: I would say on the average there are 10 students in a class. There may be considerably more than this, sometimes less, but, in my experience of teaching about 70 students and seven classes, it averages out to about 10— that seems about right.

Y: So, in your case, you teach 70 students a total of 84 hours (seven groups, 12 hours each). That's $840 you make while U.S. Reading Lab makes around $200 a student times 70, which is $14,000. They'll get a nice profit out of that.

S: I think it would be very difficult to make an estimate of their true profit.

Y: Do you have a contract with the U.S. Reading Lab, a written contract?

S: Yes, the contract specifies the salary that will be provided to me. It requires me to teach courses to the best of my ability, specifically, if I recall correctly, that I provide correct instruction in the techniques of the course. Other than that, there are no requirements or agreements regarding the number of classes that I will teach or the number of students in each class. My impression was that after teaching the first class for which I was hired, I was really not obligated to teach any further classes.

Y: Let's talk about the program. What do students learn in the program?

S: Well, what students learn really depends upon how much effort they put into the program, and in this program there are really two stages to the course. There is an initial 3-week instructional phase.

Y: Is that the length of the program—3 weeks?

S: It is 3 weeks of work on the students' part; there are four meetings.

Y: And then the program's over?

S: Right. The instructional phase terminates after four

class meetings. In that initial 3-week stage of the course, students learn how to go through reading material at rates that are between four and seven times their original reading rates—"going through" meaning being able to cover material visually in a regular, systematic, efficient way. Now "covering" may in the later parts of the course involve comprehending what they see. The emphasis initially is developing the ability to see visual material at faster rates on the assumption that once the student is able to see things at rates of, let's say 1,000 words per minute, and the necessary habits for that become truly automatic, that the comprehension will come. He'll be able to remember and understand what he sees, but he must be able to see it first. I would say in general that at the end of 3 weeks' work, students are able to read straightforward material at rates of between 800 and 1,300 words per minute with some substantial degree of comprehension. I would not say that on the average students read as well at these rates at this time as they read at their original rates of 200 or 300 words per minute, but they *are* reading to some extent. If you give them a straightforward book, they can go through it at this rate and they can tell you about it later. They may be able to describe the story in some detail up to some point and say after this point, "I really lost track of what was happening, but I remember what happened in the end," or something like that.

Y: Does the U.S. Reading Lab provide some materials that you work with?

S: Yes, the materials that are provided in the course are the basis for the reading rates that are determined.

Y: What happens after you are through teaching, after the first 3 weeks?

S: The course also entails a period of correspondence work in which students are expected to do things independently. When they complete various assignments they send in reports of these assignments to a home office. They receive back new assignments and tapes to work with. The length of time they will spend at this is about three months.

Y: Is this after the course is over?

S: This is after the instructional phase of the course. The course is presented as a 16-week program with an instructional phase and a correspondence phase. During the instructional phase students acquire the knowledge they need to become speed readers and learn how to do exercises that will develop the habits of speed reading. The actual maturation of these habits depends upon their doing the work during the correspondence section of the course.

Y: You have no idea how many students fall off and how many students continue the correspondence?

S: I really don't. My feeling on the basis of my personal experience with human nature is that a large number of students probably do not complete the program. They do not go through the 3 months of correspondence work because things interfere or because they lose interest. They've been so satisfied with the results of the first 3 weeks that they don't think it's necessary.

Y: Do you have any idea how many programs there are across the country like the one you're teaching in?

S: I could only estimate that. At any one time there are probably at least half a dozen running in each state, which would mean that there are about 300 at one time. There might be more than that; during a year's time, there are probably 12 or 15 offered at least once in different parts of each state. The goal of U.S. Reading Lab is to set up shop in each state and ultimately in foreign countries as well.

Y: How long has the U.S. Reading Lab been in business, do you know?

S: I really don't; I would guess that the parent company started operations maybe 5 years ago.

Y: Who does the promotions that appear in the paper?

S: People who are specifically hired for that. They are not necessarily teachers in the course, although they may very well have been teachers in the course at one time. In regard to their salary, I can't give you any hard numbers on that, but I have heard that they make between $1,000 and $1,500 a week.

Y: Just doing promotions?

S: Just doing the promotions. There's a lot of running around involved in that—going from place to place, setting up meetings, and doing a lot of talking with people.

Y: I see. They're not local people then?

S: Probably not.

Y: Do you think that the program is a rip-off?

S: In my mind a rip-off, a true commercial rip-off, is the sale at a high price of a product that is virtually worthless. So, for a speed-reading program to be a rip-off, it must be both high-priced and worthless. The program in which I teach is clearly expensive, not as expensive as some, but still expensive. Whether or not it has value depends on whether or not students do the work it requires and stay with it until it is completed. I make this very clear in my classes. Anyone who completes the program will be a speed reader. It might be appropriate to note that in the particular program with which I am associated no one is allowed to take the course if they have visual difficulties or if they appear to require remedial help in reading. There are screening tests for this before the course begins. Anyone, therefore, enrolled in the course is a normal reader and can expect to finish the program able to read four to seven times faster than before. Students who do not work hard enough or long enough in the program will not develop the necessary habits for speed reading, and, I suspect, will eventually read no faster than they did before the course. In this case the program *is* worthless, but it is not, of course, the program's fault. Even when students do the work and become speed readers with this program, the price tag on it may be questionable. I think, however, it may be necessary. Becoming a speed reader entails substantial work over a relatively long time, and that requires considerable motivation. In the case of most of us, it may only be by laying out $200 that we create for ourselves the necessary motivation. An interesting sidelight on all this is the fact that the speed-reading program I am affiliated with now was originally marketed as a self-study kit with tapes for $20. It didn't sell. People evidently wanted a classroom experience or simply did not believe that for $20 they would get a quality product.

Y: Do you feel ill-at-ease sharing this information with me?

S: I feel uncomfortable on this point. After having thought about this, I would not be uncomfortable sharing with you any good and true information which I have about U.S. Reading Lab or anything else. The only thing that concerns me is the possibility that the impressions that I present you with may not be entirely accurate or that they may not be truly representative because all I can

give you now are the observations that I've made personally teaching seven classes and 70 students.

Y: In the ad for the program that appears in newspapers in
every community where the program is taught, it says,
and let me just quote one part of the ad, "If you are a
student who would like to make A's instead of B's or C's,
or if you are a business person who wants to stay abreast
of today's ever changing accelerating world, then this
course is an absolute necessity." Do you think that the
U.S. Reading Lab program will improve the grades of
students in high school or college?

S: I think "will" is an awfully strong word. I think that in
this place it's inappropriate. I disagree with that kind of
verbiage in the advertising. I think that this course very
well could help a student do better in school; however, it
seems to me that the main thing in doing well in school is
studying enough and studying properly, and studying is
an entirely different thing from simply reading. We
teach certain study techniques which would be helpful,
but still doing well in school depends upon studying, and
that's different from reading.

Y: Are there any other discrepancies in the ad, in your
opinion, between what the course actually does and what
it says in the ad?

S: Yes, I think there are. Let me quote something from the
promotional material for the course. "Great Lakes Reading Lab will offer a 4-week course in speed reading to a
limited number of qualified people in the Grand Rapids
area." I think that this is an inaccurate claim in this
regard—the course is actually a 16-week program, and
people must understand that when they take the course.
If they do not understand that from the orientation
session that they receive, they will understand it, at least
in my classes, because it's one of the first things I say. It's
one of the things you have to say to give people an
accurate idea of what they're getting into.

Y: So 16 weeks instead of just 4 weeks?

S: That's right. Another quote here regarding this 4 weeks
business, "In just 4 short weeks, the average student
should be reading 4–5 times faster." I think that this
again is not an entirely accurate claim. In 4 short weeks,
the average student will not be reading four to five times
faster in the sense of feeling that he is comprehending.

NATIONALLY KNOWN SPEED READING
COURSE TO BE TAUGHT HERE IN GRAND RAPIDS

Great Lakes Reading Lab will offer a 4 week course in speed reading to a limited number of qualified people in the Grand Rapids area.

This recently developed method of instruction is the most innovative and effective program available in the United States.

Not only does this famous course reduce your time in the classroom to just one class per week for 4 short weeks, but it also includes an advanced speed reading course on cassette tape so that you can continue to improve for the rest of your life. In just 4 short weeks, the average student should be reading 4-5 times faster. In a few months some students are reading 20-30 times faster attaining speeds that approach 6,000 words per minute. In rare instances speeds of up to 13,000 wpm have been documented. Our average graduate should read 7-10 times faster upon completion of the course with marked improvement in comprehension and concentration.

For those who would like additional information, a serives of free, one hour, orientation lectures have been scheduled. At these free lectures the course will be

explained in complete detail, including classroom procedures, instructor methods, class schedule and a special 1 time only introductory tuition that is less than one third the cost of similar courses. You must attend any of the meetings for information about the Grand Rapids classes.

These orientations are open to the public, above age 14, (persons under 18 should be accompanied by a parent if possible).

If you have always wanted to be a speed reader but found the cost prohibitive or the course too time consuming ... now you can just by attending 1 evening per week for 4 short weeks you can read 7 to 10 times faster, concentrate better and comprehend more.

If you are a student who would like to make A's instead of B's or C's or if you are a business person who wants to stay abreast of today's ever changing accelerating world then this course is an absolute necessity.

These special one-hour lectures will be held at the following times and places:

ALL MEETINGS WILL BE HELD AT THE HOLIDAY INN NORTH 270 Ann St.

WED., NOV. 3	THURS., NOV. 4	FRI., NOV. 5	SAT., NOV. 6	SUN., NOV. 7	MON., NOV. 8
6:30 P.M. & 8:30 P.M.	6:30 P.M. & 8:30 P.M.	6:30 P.M. & 8:30 P.M.	2:30 P.M. & 4:30 P.M.	2:30 P.M. & 4:30 P.M.	6:30 P.M. & 8:30 P.M.

If you are a businessman, student, housewife or executive this course, which took 5 years of intensive research to develop, is a must. You can read 7-10 times faster, comprehend more, concentrate better, and remember longer. Students are offered an additional discount. This course can be taught to industry or civic groups at "group rates" upon request. Be sure to attend whichever free orientation that fits best in your schedule.

Students at the end of 4 short weeks will indeed be reading four to seven times faster than they did originally; however, their feeling of reading will not be the same as it was originally. They will not feel that they are reading in the sense that they have always understood that term—reading.

Y: Their eyes are moving faster, but they might not be reading and comprehending?

S: Yes, their eyes are moving faster and they are comprehending to some degree; however, they are not comprehending to the same degree that they would ordinarily. This is the difference, and they will know that. Almost all of them will feel that they are not reading as well at the end of the course as they do ordinarily. And so if they start the course believing that they're going to be reading as well at the end of 4 weeks as they do ordinarily, they're going to be disappointed. And it's unreasonable theoretically to expect that speed reading is something that you can acquire in 3 weeks' work and four lessons. In my courses students do not do the course with the expectation of being able to read four to five times faster, just as well at the end of 3 weeks' work. I make this as clear as I can.

Y: Even though it says that in the ad?

S: Even though it says it in the ad, so that if anyone were to be misled by the ad or by anything they would hear during the orientation session, they should get the true information on the first night of the course. I try to make as clear as I can the requirements of the course in the long term and what it really takes in my view to become a speed reader. Occasionally, one student will say that he can't invest that much time or he really doesn't have that much interest; these people get their money back. One thing about this course is that any student can get his money back at any time just by asking for it.

Y: Is it on a prorated basis?

S: I'm not sure; it may depend upon the reasons.

Y: I would guess that if they went to three classes out of four they wouldn't get their entire fee back.

S: They might, though.

Y: Are there any other things in the ad that bother you?

S: Yes, there's a grosser exaggeration along the same lines a little further on. Here it says, ". . . just by attending 1 evening per week for 4 short weeks you can read 7 to 10

times faster, concentrate better and comprehend more."
I think that this would probably give a misleading
impression. At the end of 4 weeks you can't read seven to
ten times faster; at least you will not feel that you are
reading seven to ten times faster. At the end of the
course this is a real possibility, the course being 16 weeks
long, not 4. The other discrepancy I think between the
promotion and the reality of the course is the remark
about making better grades in school, which we already
discussed.

Y: Is that about it on the ad?

S: Yes.

Y: What are your general opinions about the course? I
know you've said a lot of them already, but after you've
taught seven classes for about 70 students and we've
talked about it, what are your general impressions about
taking and teaching a speed-reading course? Do you
think it's possible to read 1,000 words per minute on any
kind of material and remember what you've read?

S: I think that it's possible to read 1,000 words per minute
on straightforward material.

Y: How do you define straightforward material?

S: Straightforward material would be, in my mind, narrative reading with a relatively uncomplicated plot with
relatively ordinary vocabulary without any really complicated thinking or reasoning required of the people
who read it. An example would be any story by John
Steinbeck or Ernest Hemingway. A more complicated,
less straightforward kind of reading would be narrative
material of the sort written by Robert Penn Warren.
Unstraightforward material would be any kind of technical material crammed with facts possibly involving
rather difficult reasoning.

Y: Which kinds of materials do students and businessmen
read more of—uncomplicated, straightforward material
or the more complicated material, in your opinion?

S: I think it depends on what area of business or what area
of scholarship a person spends most of his time with. I
would say many people, if not most people, spend most
of their time reading fairly complicated material. My
feeling about speed-reading complicated material is that
if it is truly possible to read through complicated material four or five times the original reading rate, and
comprehend it just as well, that speed reading is a skill

that most of us would find useful. But few of us would be able to read that fast without the techniques and the discipline of a formal course. Becoming a speed reader is a matter of erasing the habits that make us slow readers and developing habits of pacing and eye control and reading directly that will allow us to read many times faster. The process is necessarily a slow one and one that requires sustained effort and regular practice. Both commercial and nonprofit programs in speed reading will in most cases provide efficient instruction in techniques for effective speed reading. The particular value in my mind of commercial programs is that they may run longer (for months instead of weeks, and therefore may be more successful in turning knowledge of techniques into habits—there is a real difference between knowing about a skill and being able to execute it fully automatically; being able to do this takes practice and time) and, because of what they cost, may provide the incentive required to stay with a program long enough for it to pay off.

Y: Are you required to do any promotional work for the company in your teaching?

S: No.

Y: I think that covers what I wanted to know. I really appreciate your sharing the information with me.

S: You're welcome.

At the 1976 meeting of the National Reading Conference in Atlanta several proponents and opponents of speed-reading merchandising were present. Dr. Ronald Carver of the University of Missouri at Kansas City delivered a research report on his theory of reading comprehension called "rauding," a combination of comprehension in listening and reading.[4] He would measure reading speed on the basis of how many sentences or thoughts a person read per minute. Carver claims that neither studying nor skimming can be called reading because the reader is not comprehending consecutive sentences while studying or skimming. I agree with him. Many speed-reading courses teach skimming techniques and such study techniques as reading the first sentence of paragraphs and summaries before reading a selection. The students of speed-reading courses are led to believe they are reading more efficiently as a result of learning to move their eyes faster.

At the Atlanta convention there was discussion among the secondary and college reading-study skills specialists present that the teaching of speed reading at the college level might be a waste of time. The idea was proposed that by the time one is 18 years old, one has established one's reading rate, and that any attempt to increase that rate of reading would result in a decrease of reading efficiency or comprehension. Some professors agreed that people tend to zero in on their most efficient reading rate after a number of years of reading, roughly by age 18; that is not to say that it might not be 15 or 21. There is also some evidence[5] that it might be a waste of time to teach adults to be flexible readers, that is, to read materials of different levels of difficulty and interest at varying rates of speed. The study I completed in 1967[6] with over 3,000 adult college students indicated that college students were indeed flexible readers. Whether speed reading and flexible reading are practiced or valuable is a highly individual concern, in my opinion. I think it is important for anyone who has not taken a speed-reading course to realize how easy it is to increase one's reading speed. Most people do read everything at the same rate—the newspaper, an important paper at work, and the back of the cereal box at breakfast. Following is a simple exercise you can complete which should give you confidence that you can increase your reading speed by just deciding to do so. Your comprehension or efficiency level is much more of an individual matter, however.

Following is a timed reading exercise. This is an excerpt from the speed-reading chapter of my book, *Surviving in College,* [7] a study-skills program for high school and college students. Time yourself for 1 minute. Note the line number you are on at the end of 1 minute.

	Start timing yourself and read:
1	Did you ever think that improving your reading
2	speed is just a matter of habit, that
3	is, breaking old ones and beginning new ones?
4	In the case of Paul in the story
5	above, he had easily got into the habit
6	of reading things slowly word by word because
7	he was always taking math, physics, or engineering
8	courses that required word-by-word slow reading.
9	He was rewarded in these classes by getting
10	As for his careful work, However, when he
11	got into a class that required fast reading
12	for an entirely different purpose, he was not
13	able to be flexible and adjust his reading
14	speed to his purpose—that is, read a
15	lot faster and disregard the details. Paul found
16	out about a book on speed reading and

17	with some practice he found that he could
18	read easy material at 500 words per minute,
19	and when he took a comprehension test afterwards
20	he found that he could still remember the
21	main ideas with at least 80 percent accuracy.
22	Now Paul's friend Mary was a different case
23	entirely. Mary had some vocabulary and word-analysis
24	problems when she first started college. She tried
25	the speed reading bit and just went from
26	bad to worse. She found out right away
27	that when you have problems recognizing words, pronouncing
28	new words, and not knowing the meanings of
29	some words, speed reading is *not* for you.
30	If you don't know the meanings of words,
31	it doesn't matter how fast you read—you're
32	going to run into trouble. So if you
33	don't have any vocabulary problems or basic skills
34	problems, then speed reading is a skill you
35	can practice, but if you do have vocabulary
36	problems, forget it. Usually speed-reading courses use
37	expensive machines that flash reading selections on a
38	screen at a line at a time. The
39	speed can be controlled from 200 to 1,000
40	words per minute. There are also devices available
41	that you place over the book you are
42	reading which have some sort of shutter or
43	bar which moves slowly down the page. Your
44	job is to keep your eyes moving ahead
45	of the "pacer." Another speed-reading method that
46	is taught is the use of the hand
47	as a pacer. By moving your hand slowly
48	down the page with your fingers outstretched and
49	by keeping your hand constantly moving you can
50	keep your eyes moving faster back and forth,
51	left to right and back down the page.
52	Another speed-reading technique is to teach students
53	to carefully and slowly read the table of
54	contents, the introduction, the first chapter, and the
55	last chapter. Then as the student speed reads
56	the chapters, the student is instructed to slow
57	down and carefully read the first and last
58	paragraphs of every chapter while flying through the
59	other paragraphs skipping words, sentences, and sometimes whole

60   paragraphs as the eyes scan and skim at
61   a terrific rate, not seeing every word. When
62   this technique is used, the resulting rate in
63   words per minute can be astronomical, in the
64   thousands. But to say that it is a
65   reading rate in words per minute is a
66   lie. Anyone can turn the pages of a
67   book as fast as he can and claim
68   that he read the book by seeing a
69   few words on each page. Add to that
70   the careful reading of the first and last
71   paragraph of each chapter and naturally one would
72   remember or learn a few things about the
73   book. But to say that you read the
74   book is as phony as saying that you've
75   seen a movie after reading a review of
76   it. Reading is seeing every word; there's no
77   getting around that fact, especially college reading.

Figure out your reading speed by multiplying by eight the line you stopped on after 1 minute. Write your speed here:

A. _____ words per minute

Now go back and finish reading through line 77. We can assume that reading rate A (above) is your normal reading rate—give or take 100 words per minute, since it's a crude estimate based on only 1 minute with no instructions about *how* to read the selection.

You read a little bit about speed reading in the selection you just finished. The major point was that reading is seeing every word and that if you are going to increase your reading speed, you are going to have to increase your speed of seeing every word! And that *can* be done—up to a point. Simply by telling yourself you are going to read much, much faster, seeing every word—you can. On the next selection, make up your mind that you are going to read twice as fast as you did on the first selection. Consciously zoom your eyes across the page trying not to read word by word with your "inner voice," saying the words "aloud" inside your head. Move your eyes quickly across the words concentrating on the meaning, on moving rapidly, and on not stopping or going back (regressing). Occasionally, in the selection you will see the sentence, "Read faster!" This is to remind you to continue to move your eyes quickly.

You are to time yourself for 1 minute as you did on the first selection. At the end of 1 minute note the line number you are on. Remember to read as rapidly as you can. Start timing yourself and read:

1   There is no doubt that if you want
2   to read faster you can do it. The
3   speed-reading ads promise that you will get
4   your money back if you do not double
5   your reading speed. Well, if your beginning reading
6   rate is around 150 or 200 words per
7   minute, it is quite easy to double your
8   reading speed to 300 or 400 words per
9   minute just by saying to yourself, "I want
10 to read faster," and consciously trying to do
11 it. Concentrate on trying to read fast every
12 time you are reading easy material which is
13 appropriate for speed-reading techniques. Actually, most of
14 us are lazy, slow readers. It is said
15 that the average reading speed of most adults,
16 including college graduates, is 250 words per minute,
17 which is very slow. It is possible, when
18 defining reading as seeing every word, to read
19 as fast as 600 to 900 words per
20 minute. Read faster! Of course, it isn't easy
21 to remember to read faster every time you
22 read. We have been conditioned to read slowly
23 through 12 years of schooling. One cannot
24 break out of the slow reading habit built
25 up over that many years in just 1
26 day. You need to practice to break such
27 ingrained habits. That is why the speed-reading
28 merchants with their $300 to $500 courses are
29 so successful. If you pay that much money
30 for someone to teach you to speed-read
31 chances are you will learn to speed-read.
32 What the speed-reading courses actually do is
33 to force you to practice moving your eyes
34 rapidly over the page. Read faster! However, you
35 can practice on your own, using your hand
36 or a 3 × 5 card as a pacer if
37 you wish, simply by making up your mind
38 that you want to learn to break the
39 slow word-by-word reading habit and read
40 faster. You will be amazed at your reading
41 speed on this selection, achieved simply by telling
42 yourself to read faster without any practice at
43 all. This demonstration should be enough evidence for
44 you to realize that speed reading is all

45	in your head—it's a matter of practice
46	and habit. If you want to do it
47	you can, without paying someone $400 to teach
48	you how to do it. By the way,
49	if you do happen to double your reading
50	speed on this selection, just drop your check
51	for $400 into any mailbox to the author.
52	Just kidding, of course, but isn't it ridiculous
53	for people to pay that much money for
54	a speed-reading course when they can do
55	it on their own for free? Actually there
56	is even a better way to do it
57	in this program. The author of this book
58	has written some "words of wisdom" on the
59	topic of speed reading which you probably ought
60	to read. Then he has put together several
61	learning alternatives which can help you break the
62	slow old word-by-word habit. Some of
63	the exercises include the use of the controlled
64	reader, a machine which forces you to read
65	faster. Other exercises are workbooks which include timed
66	reading selections which include questions at the end
67	which check your conprehension. Speed reading is really
68	a bad label for faster reading because what
69	you are really after is faster comprehension. We
70	probably ought to call it "speed comprehension." What
71	good is reading faster if you can't remember
72	anything you have read? So most of the
73	learning alternatives include practice material with questions at
74	the end. A general rule of thumb is
75	that if you can answer 70 percent of
76	the questions correctly after speed reading, you have
77	shown good comprehension.

Now multiply by eight the line you stopped on at the end of 1 minute. If you reached the end of the selection before 1 minute went by, you were reading faster than 600 words per minute, which is fast enough. Write your speed here:

         B. _____ words per minute

If you doubled your reading speed, you should now be aware of how easy it is to learn to read faster. It is a matter of attitude or motivation. If you want to, you can.

References

1. Smith, Frank, *Comprehension and Learning,* Holt, Rinehart and Winston, New York, 1975.
2. Cattell, James, "Ueber die Zeit der Erkennung und Benennung von Schriftzeichen, Bildern und Farben," *Philosophische Studien,* vol. 2, 1885, pp. 635–650, translated and reprinted in *James McKeen Cattell, Man of Science,* 1860–1944 (vol. 1), Science Press, Lancaster, Pa., 1947.
3. Pauk, Walter, "Reading and Living," unpublished manuscript, Ithaca, N.Y., 1960.
4. Carver, Ronald P., "Measuring Prose Difficulty Using the Rauding Scale," *Reading Research Quarterly,* vol. 11, No. 4, 1975–1976, pp. 660–685.
5. Yarington, D. J., "Some Second Thoughts on Teaching Flexibility," in *Proceedings on the 11th Annual Conference,* The College Reading Association, 1967.
6. Yarington, D. J., *A Study of the Relationships between the Reading Done by College Freshmen and Aptitude and Scholastic Achievement,* U.S. Department of Health, Education and Welfare, Office of Education, Cooperative Research Project, 5-8421, ERIC number EDU13-712, 1967.
7. Yarington, D. J., *Surviving in College,* The Bobbs-Merrill Co., Inc., Indianapolis, 1977, pp. 39–44.

TEN

THE BOTTOM LINE: FOR PARENTS ONLY

Whether schools are joyless and oppressive as they are described by Charles Silberman in *Crisis in the Classroom*,[1] whether they are places where professional teachers are unsuccessfully fighting for their rights as they are described by Myron Brenton in *What's Happened to Teacher?*,[2] whether they are places that practice the "art of savage discovery" or how to blame failure on the victim as William Ryan describes in *Blaming the Victim*,[3] or whether they adequately educate a minority of children depends upon one's point of view. Many parents are satisfied with schools as they are. But at its simplest, school is as good as the teacher your child has right now. You be the judge. A list of some of the titles published since 1970 gives an indication of the negative publicity schools have been getting: *Deschooling Society*,[4] *Students! Do Not Push Your Teacher down the Stairs on Friday*,[5] *The Real Teachers*,[6] *Free the Children*,[7] *How to Survive in Your Native Land*,[8] and *How to Change the Schools, A Parents' Action Handbook on How to Fight the System*.[9] Schools have been under tremendous pressure to reform partially as a result of these books. Cornelius Troost has edited a rejoinder to the radical school reform movement,[10] a collection of essays admitting shortcomings in the schools, but providing traditional "within-the-system" solutions. The essayists include Jonathan Kozol on free schools, Sidney Hook on deschooling society, and Fred Hechinger on Summerhill.

Parents are powerless. By the time they realize that their schools are in need of improvement and work hard for some small changes, their children have usually gone on to middle school, junior high, high school, work, or college. Teachers and administrators who recognize the need for change also feel powerless, as do boards of education.

If you walked into the school your child attends, what evidence would there be that the school fits the descriptions in this book? Following is an attitude checklist with explanations and questions at the end of each explanation. Take the questions to your child's school, and using your own information-gathering techniques (talking to the principal, talking to teachers, talking to kids, observing classes and classrooms) find out how many of the attitudes are present. Think about what you can do to change them. This is just a partial checklist. You can form questions from any of the topics in the previous chapters. Following are discussions of eight attitudes.

Television Is Bad for Kids

Teachers generally are blind to the impact of the most powerful medium of communication in our society—television. Every child in school today is a person who has been brought up on television. By the time the average student graduates from high school, he or she has spent only 11,000 hours in school, but more than 22,000 hours watching television. Many students claim they learn much more from TV than they do from school. Granted, considering the educational *potential* of television, most present programming provides an educational wasteland, but to say that all TV shows are "bad" for kids is naive. For example, "Sesame Street," "The Electric Company," and "Mister Rogers' Neighborhood," three well-known shows for children, have had a tremendous positive impact that has been well-documented. The USOE and the Ford, Mobil, and Carnegie Foundations have invested millions of dollars each year to fund the Children's Television Workshop to produce such shows. Each show has made mistakes and they are easy to point to, but no one can deny that all three are better than any previous children's shows. New children's shows are added each year by the networks, and they continue to improve.

Children arrive in kindergarten or 1st grade having watched these shows daily for as many as 4 years. The dull, seats-in-a-row teaching that they encounter does not begin to compete with the television experiences. Animated, imaginative, and creative teachers can compete with television, but most cannot. What teacher could possibly compete with Bill Cosby and a 15-million-dollar-a-year budget? And why should they want to? Schools need to realize that television can be their greatest ally, rather than their greatest threat. Children who watch the shows right in the classroom or who are encouraged to watch them at home and use the curriculum guides provided have the best of both worlds. But it has been my experience that teachers do not spend much time during the school day allowing children to watch television. I find plenty of television sets, but they are off in corners covered with dust. It is significant that the shows mentioned above are not directed by educators, but the Children's Television Workshop was very careful to involve teachers from the very beginning so that its efforts would not be boycotted by teachers. When the producers of "The Electric Company" went to teachers to get their reactions to the first year of shows, they got the reactions they expected. "True Blue Sue" was too sexy. "Easy Reader" was "too black." The music was too "loud" and too "rock." The pace was too "fast."

Television is here to stay and its impact on kids is very, very real. Its possibilities for promoting learning to read and enhancing reading are unlimited. If you want to read more about television, its impact on kids, and what parents can do about it, read a book called *Go Watch T.V.*,[11] by Nat Rutstein, who was an NBC news producer in New York. Realizing what uncontrolled watching of TV was doing to kids, he quit the network television job and took a university teaching job. His book has had a positive impact on parents and on the networks. It has been widely read in England as well as in this country.

I recently walked through schools in two school systems that have placed at least one color TV set in every school. (Some systems have placed a set in every school room.) I looked for the sets and found them collecting dust in a storage corner, obviously not used. I am not advocating the replacement of teachers by TV sets. I do feel, however, that television and videotaped shows recorded for use when the teacher wants them can be enormously valuable. If a child is hooked on TV, for example, and hates reading, why not use television to get her interested in reading a book? If teachers can use television as an interest-getting device, a starting point, then a real alliance can be made between TV and the classroom.

Question: Does your school use television to facilitate learning and reading?

Reading Is Good, in and of Itself

This is probably one of the most pervasive attitudes in schools. The idea that reading is intrinsically good in and of itself eliminates the need to read for a purpose. If reading teachers continue to place reading on a pedestal and continue to pretend that they own the answers in reading, then their safety in their positions is maintained—so long as no one asks some serious questions. And that is exactly what has happened. A by-product of this is the fact that most of the time spent in school on reading is spent on the process of learning to read. Not much time is spent on the uses of reading, that is, meeting various needs like learning, gaining information, and enjoying. After the 5th grade, right on through college, few teachers are concerned with reading, unless the students have a problem with the process of knowing how to read. Teachers above the 5th grade expect children to know how to comprehend reading materials in social studies, math, science, and other content areas.

   Question: Are all the teachers in the school concerned with the uses of reading?

Time in School Equals Proficiency in Reading

Question: "Do you speak French?"
   Answer: "I had 7 years of it."
Question: "How well do you read?"
   Answer: "I took a speed-reading course."
Question: "Do you know about the Civil War?"
   Answer: "We had a 3-week unit on it in American History 273."

   None of these typical answers responds to the questions, but all reinforce the idea that time-in-school equals learning. The U.S. Census has reported literacy data by reporting the number of years of school completed by individuals, as if going to school equals learning to read! It's like asking your child's teacher how well your child reads and having the teacher respond that the child is reading at the 4.5-grade level. What that really means I don't know, but if the child is in the 4th grade, parents are usually satisfied with the answer. If the child is in the 8th grade, parents get very angry because they *expect* time in school to result in learning to read. Clearly the *time* spent in school means nothing, but the fact that parents expect time in school to equal learning is indicated by a lawsuit filed in California on behalf of an 18-year-old graduate of Galileo High School in San Francisco. The suit alleged that the student graduated from high school with a 4th-grade reading level and was therefore unable to read or fill out a job application. The case is known as the *Peter Doe* case. The question raised was: Are schools liable for nonlearning? Should we expect children to learn during the time spent in school? Stephen Sugarman, a law professor at the University of California, compared other professions like law and medicine to teaching in explaining the *Peter Doe* case. The case is like a malpractice suit in medicine.

      . . . the school could not avoid liability simply by claiming that
      schools promise opportunities, not results. What it boils down

to is that while a doctor (or school) is not legally required to ensure that the client will get well (or learn) once he (or it) undertakes to treat (or teach), there is a professional obligation to do so.[12]

The case has since been thrown out of court, but this was just the first one. Other such cases are appearing all over the country as parents are discovering their kids are graduating without having survival literacy skills.

Question: Do children spend time in your school without learning to read?

There Is One Best Method of Teaching Reading

After years of controversy over methodology, reading specialists have recently agreed that there is no one best method. There is a best method for *each child,* and there are enough alternative approaches to teaching reading to match each child's individual needs and aptitudes. Therefore, the teacher's role as diagnostician and facilitator of learning becomes vital. Each child has certain aptitudes and skills, and the teacher's job is one of matching appropriate methods and materials to these abilities. This trial-and-error approach provides a means of finding the best method for teaching reading to each child. The teacher simply "tries out" different books, materials, stories, and teaching techniques until the child responds in a positive enough way for the teacher to say, "This is the approach that works with this child." Unfortunately, 95 percent of the elementary schools in the country use one of the basal-reader systems (sets of graded readers) as the major approach to teaching reading. In many schools, the basal-reader system used is a set of readers published 15 or 20 years ago, before some of the publishers caught on to the idea of making the books colorful and full of exciting stories relevant to the backgrounds of the children. It is sad but true that many schools *still* use the old "Dick and Jane" or "Alice and Jerry" readers. They say they simply cannot afford to pay for new books or alternative sets of materials.

Any school system that uses one approach and one set of materials for *all* children does not recognize the concept of individual differences among children. We all have different learning styles, aptitudes, and interests.

Question: Does your school system provide several alternative methods and materials for facilitating learning to read?

Materials Teach Reading

Ask a teacher how your child is doing in reading and she may say, "Well, he's reading in the 2.1 book now," as if the book was teaching him to read. Teachers often complain about not having time to cover the materials, as if the materials did the teaching. Nowhere is Carl Roger's concept on *facilitating* learning more appropriate than in the area of reading.[13] Those children who learn to read do so because they were facilitated, helped, taught by a human being—not a basal reader, workbook, machine, or trade book. The teacher provided the kinds of materials, practice activities, learning environment, and the *direct instruction* which facilitated learning to read. Children are highly motivated to read. Many children learn to read before they arrive at school. They learned by themselves or with a parent, peer, brother, or sister. Most children learn to read in school despite the dull materials, despite a dull affective environment, and despite the teacher. Children need facilitation or assistance, not just materials, which according to some teachers seem magically to do the job for them.

Facilitation implies assistance, cooperation, and learning, things materials cannot do alone.

Question: In the classrooms in your school do teachers assume that materials teach?

Teachers Are Equal in Ability, or a Reading Teacher Is a Reading Teacher Is a Reading Teacher

As noted earlier, a commonly held belief in schools is that if Billie has Mrs. Jones for 3rd grade and Sally has Mrs. Smith for 3rd grade, both are getting 3rd grade. Not true. Billie is getting Mrs. Jones and Sally is getting Mrs. Smith. No more, no less. The same is true in reading. The reading that your son or daughter gets is as good as the teacher teaching it. To say that reading teachers are interchangeable is ridiculous.

Teacher colleges perpetuate this attitude with time-in-course recommendations for reading-specialist certification. Hopefully, they think, if all reading teachers take the same courses, they will be the same.

Question: Are the teachers in your school equal in abilities?

Follow-ups: Who are the good teachers? Why are they better? Do your children get the good teachers? Who does? Who doesn't? Why?

Reading Is Taught during the Reading Period

READING PERIOD, SECOND GRADE
A 15-Minute Vignette

It is 9 A.M. and there are 26 children in the classroom (7 black, 19 white) sitting in rows at desks. The teacher (T) has just finished opening exercises with the children.

T: It's time for reading now. Will the Bluebirds bring chairs to the reading corner? (Eight children noisily pick up chairs and carry them to a corner of the room.)

T: Quietly, children. (They seat themselves in a circle.)

T: Okay, Sallie, go ahead.

Sallie: As Sam and Martha walked in the cave, Sam led. He was the bravest of the two. Martha was timid in the darkness.

T: Who can tell me what timid means? (To the rest of the class.) Frank, John isn't back there to visit with you. Mary, pick up the pencil.

T: Yes, Bob.

Bob: Timid is when you're scared. Girls get scared in the dark.

T: Yes, that's right. That's fine; now, Paul. (While Paul reads, the teacher stands and walks around the classroom.)

T: There's a little too much visiting. You're not working if you're talking. (She walks back to the reading corner.)

T: Fine, Paul; now, Steve.

Steve: Mrs. Collins shurdered . . .

T: Shuddered (correcting him).

Steve: As she opened the door. Somethin'. . .

Bob: Something.

T: We have to figure these words out ourselves. Bob, don't help. Okay, Frank, you're next.

Frank: (Reads)

T: Now, Robins, get out your workbooks. Sparrows, get ready to come up. (A boy brings his workbook to the teacher and she shows him the correct page.)

T: Fine, Frank; now, Molly.

Frank: Molly is sick today.

T: Okay, children. Bluebirds back to your desks. Page 18 in your workbooks. Sparrows next. Quietly now. (Seven black children carry chairs and books to the reading corner.)

This is a typical look into a 2nd-grade classroom. A "hidden curriculum" is being taught every day in almost every classroom in the country. The above example is contrived in order to include three of the lessons of the hidden curriculum during the reading period. Practice exercises in reading aloud are taking place. (The children are often ridiculed for making mistakes. By the way, when was the last time you read aloud without making a mistake?) The teacher's major concern, however, is classroom discipline: a quiet classroom is a good classroom. The first lesson of the reading period is to be quiet and sit still.

Lesson number two in the hidden curriculum of the reading period is the sexism of the graded basal readers. As discussed in Chap. 6, such notions as girls are timid or weak; it's not ladylike to win; girls are passive, docile, and dependent; girls can only be in certain jobs like nursing and waiting on tables; and a woman's place is in the home are stereotypes that children learn during the reading period through the graded basal readers. Books such as *Dick and Jane as Victims, Sex Stereotyping in Children's Readers*[14] and *Sexism in School and Society*[15] document this not-so-subtle indoctrination. There is some evidence that publishers are responding to the accusations of sexism, but only after some have been taken to court.

> Since federal funds help to pay for textbooks, it is argued that school boards using sexist texts may be sued under Title IX of the Education Amendments Act of 1972, which forbids sex discrimination in federally funded educational programs. The first such suit was brought last May in Michigan by a group called the Committee to Study Sex Discrimination in the Kalamazoo Public Schools. After studying twelve readers for Grades 1 through 6, the committee filed a complaint with the Department of Health, Education and Welfare. The complaint alleges, among other charges, that 80% of the leading characters in the reading series are boys or men, that the pronoun "she" is not introduced in the pre-primer series until the third volume, that women are "portrayed predominately as mothers, nurses, librarians, storekeepers . . ."
>
> Publishers are facing comparable pressures in Brookline, Mass., Detroit, Seattle, Dallas, Atlanta and New York City. Major textbook packagers such as Ginn, Silver Burdett, Houghton, Mifflin, Harper & Row and Scott, Foresman have all been singled out. And there are indications that some of them have begun thinking about costly reform projects to eliminate stereotyping, just as they have already expunged, in some cases, editorial sins against blacks.[16]

Both McGraw-Hill and Scott, Foresman have since published guidelines for their authors.

The third lesson of the hidden curriculum during the reading period is racism. The separation of black and white children within each classroom is often accomplished through grouping for reading— the Sparrows are the low group. The demeaning nature in which blacks and other minority groups are treated in graded basal readers and in classrooms has already been discussed.

That reading is not the only thing taught during the reading period is a fact that has been overlooked for years. The publishers and teacher-education institutions are beginning to respond with new publications and new teacher training to deal with attitudes and stereotyping. But what about the millions of *old* readers still in use in schools and what about the millions of teachers who have been "successful" with those readers? And what about teachers who are not aware of their hidden curriculum?

Question: What is taught during the reading period in your school?

Children Must Read to Learn

Learning to read is a survival skill needed by children in our society, perhaps needed most by minority children. Nevertheless, the idea that children *must* learn to read in order to learn is erroneous. Although it is widely assumed that if a child does not learn to read he will not learn anything in school, as society becomes more and more visually and multimedia oriented and less literacy oriented, the need for reading well will lessen. Reading will, no doubt, always be the highest priority medium for learning, but television, radio, movies, listening, experiencing signs and symbols in the community, etc., are just some of the other media through which learning takes place. After children have achieved a survival literacy level or a level at which they can read directions, signs, newspapers, and other survival-type literature, they may see little need for reading. If a child rejects reading, that does not signal the end of her learning for the rest of her life. Books will never be obsolete as a learning medium, but they may very well lessen in degree of importance.

Question: In how many different ways do children learn in your school?

Summary

The above list of questions on prevailing attitudes may be a starting point for your learning what really goes on in your child's school. Because every school is different, I strongly encourage you to investigate the one that teaches and influences your children. Ask questions, look at the cumulative records of your child, interview the principal, attend school-board meetings. Get involved and get information. Then decide what you can do about it. Share the information with your friends. Group action is often more powerful than an individual's.

References

1. Silberman, Charles E., *Crisis in the Classroom,* Random House, New York, 1970.
2. Brenton, Myron, *What's Happened to Teacher?,* Avon Books, New York, 1970.
3. Ryan, William, *Blaming the Victim,* Vintage Books, New York, 1971.
4. Illich, Ivan, *Deschooling Society,* Harper & Row, New York, 1970.
5. Jones, Alan, *Students! Do Not Push Your Teacher down the Stairs on Friday,* Penguin Books, New York, 1972.
6. Sterling, Philip (editor), *The Real Teachers,* Vintage Books, New York, 1972.
7. Graubard, Allen, *Free the Children,* Random House, New York, 1972.
8. Herndon, James, *How to Survive in Your Native Land,* Simon & Schuster, New York, 1971.
9. Lurie, Ellen, *How to Change the Schools, A Parents' Action Handbook on How to Fight the System,* Vintage Books, New York, 1970.
10. Troost, Cornelius J. (editor), *Radical School Reform —Critique and Alternatives,* Little, Brown and Co., Boston, 1973.
11. Rutstein, Nathan, *Go Watch T.V.,* Sheed and Ward, New York, 1974.
12. Sugarman, Stephen D., "If Johnnie Can't Read—Get Yourself a Lawyer," *Learning,* vol. 2, No. 8, April 1974, p. 28.
13. Rogers, Carl, *Freedom to Learn,* Charles E. Merrill Publishing Co., Columbus, Ohio, 1969.
14. *Dick and Jane as Victims, Sex Stereotyping in Children's Readers,* Women on Words & Images, Princeton, N.J. 1972.
15. Frazier, Nancy, and Sadker, Myra, *Sexism in School and Society,* Harper & Row, Inc., New York, 1973.
16. "Sexist Texts," *Time Magazine,* November 5, 1973.

ELEVEN

SOME ALTERNATIVES

"So what?" my friend asked. "You've told us about this complex Machine and claimed that you understand the problem and you're asking the right questions. If *you* don't have any answers, who does?" He's right; it would be irresponsible of me to finish this book without suggesting some alternatives.

Immediate Partial Solutions

There are some seemingly easy partial solutions. A quick review of the wrongheaded attitudes examined in Chap. 10 suggests some immediate answers. What would schools look like if these attitudes were not present?

Television. There would be a television set in every classroom, being used imaginatively by a teacher who combines the regular content with television shows. More extensive use is fairly easy. For example, the local television station could provide taped replays of evening programs during the day. If the school is on a cable system, rerunning tapes would be easier. More extensive use can also be expensive: Several high schools have their own closed-circuit television system where any teacher can order a pretaped program or movie for any class.

Using reading. The school principal seems to be the person who has the power to place more emphasis on *using* reading skills than on simply teaching reading skills. Programs for principals which explain to them methods of teaching reading in all the different content areas would be helpful. Reading science is different from reading math, reading math is different from reading social studies, and so on. Schools where children and students read for fun, where time is specifically set aside each day for reading, are usually schools where the leader (the principal) is hooked on reading.

Time in school equals reading proficiency. This is a myth that has been exploded by several court cases holding the schools accountable for teaching and learning in schools. We all know that time in school does not necessarily result in learning—at the college level as well. It would be a dubious educational innovation to suggest a test to graduate from elementary school or high school, but several states are suggesting just that. The solution is to require all levels of school to be accountable for the learning they promise.

There is one best method of teaching reading. If every teacher in every elementary school had available at least 10 different sets of materials for teaching reading, representing 10 different methods of teaching (and this would be at no additional cost to the community—just fewer editions of each kind of material), we could cut our illiteracy rate in half. If every teacher attempted to determine each child's learning style and to match that to a method and set of materials for learning to read, then the teacher would be seeking the best method (or methods) for that particular child.

Teachers teach reading. In the literature on humanistic education, which is growing every day (a 29-book list is provided at the end of this chapter), there are literally hundreds of suggestions for facilitating a positive, warm, loving, and caring classroom climate.

Teachers are equal. Teachers aren't any more equal than are doctors and lawyers, although doctors and lawyers are subjected to much more stringent standards for entry into their professions than teachers are. The hiring, firing, and tenure policies of the local schools are the places where quality control must be maintained, and the teachers' unions do not appear to be very interested in maintaining quality. They are more interested in maintaining the status quo for more and more salary.

Reading is taught. The hidden curriculum, or the shadow curriculum as it is sometimes called, is an illusive devil. Many teachers aren't even aware of the racism, sexism, and docility that they are teaching. How do we eliminate it? Awareness of the problem is step number one. Changing attitudes is probably step two. I don't know how to do that in almost every classroom in America.

Children must read to learn. Children learn from every life experience. Again, this is a problem of teacher and school attitudes and philosophies. The answer is in teacher training.

Teacher Training

The above review of the wrongheaded attitudes pervasive in schools only suggests immediate Band-Aid solutions. To bring about lasting positive changes, I believe the training of teachers is the point at which schools and children ultimately can be influenced the most. The elimination of such social ills as crime, violence, and racism is often laid at the doorstep of education when the judicial and other systems fail to produce changes. The thinking is that perhaps if we start with educating very young children, things will be different in the future. They won't be different until we change the system of educating the teachers who teach the children. Schools reflect our society, as I have pointed out, and new teachers reflect society as much as the old ones. Yet, teacher education seems to me to be the best place to start. Each of the eight preceding statements are changes that could be brought about by a new breed of teachers—teachers who care about making changes, and who know how to do it. I believe it is entirely possible to train teachers who wear invisible bands on their arms that say, "I give a damn."

The three most powerful innovations in teacher education are humanistic education, competency-based education, and values education.

Humanistic education. Humanizing teacher-education classrooms and humanizing prospective teachers are accomplished simultaneously. Teachers are apt to teach the way they were taught, so we are told by research on teacher education. With declining enrollments in colleges and universities and with the shift in interest of students from the traditional liberal arts or the humanities to the more practical areas of business and social science, college faculties are being forced to change for survival. "Faculty development" programs are emerging in a time of retrenchment. Faculty members are being asked to teach different topics and are being asked to teach in different ways. The old lecture, read-the-textbook, take-the-test method of college teaching is coming under fire. What a threat to the Ph.D.s, most of whom never had any training at all in teaching. Traditionally, college professors have taught the way they were taught. If faculty development programs (in-service programs for the retraining of college teachers) could retrain college professors to be more humanistic, then the effect on prospective teachers would be tremendous, for teacher-education courses are not the only college courses taken by prospective teachers.

Making classrooms more humanistic means making them more people-oriented. In the case of teacher education, that means putting teacher education where the teachers are—out in the schools where the people are. It also means making the teaching–learning process relevant to the lives of the teachers in training and relevant to the real issues of society. The lecture/textbook/test method is the opposite of a humanistically oriented teacher-education program. In a humanistically oriented teacher-education program, we don't talk about it, we do it. At the end of this chapter is a list of books in the ever-growing literature on humanistic education. The one by Carl Rogers *(Freedom to Learn)* expresses best the concept of facilitating positive, humanistic classroom environments.

Competence. Parents have assumed for years that if a teacher has graduated from a teacher-training institution, she or he is competent to teach, much the same as a student who graduates from high school is expected to be able to read. We don't need much more data to indicate that the former is as false as the latter. The competency-based teacher-education (CBTE) movement is a step in the right direction.

CBTE, although not an outgrowth of behavioristic psychology, has behavioristic psychologists as its most enthusiastic proponents. The behaviorists say, "Show me an observable behavior and I will show you a way to measure it." Ten years ago, at the beginning of the CBTE movement, everyone agreed that teacher training should be based on teacher performance rather than course credit. Traditionally, the only way to judge a beginning teacher was to look at the college transcript to see what courses the teacher took and the grades received, grades, which as we know, can be very arbitrary and vary from professor to professor. A college transcript tells us the teacher spent time in the course and "learned" an "A" or a "B." Time-in-course standards were used for years for certifying and hiring teachers. Certain numbers of credit hours in certain courses are required by state certification agencies. Teachers were hired based on recommendations, grades, where they went to college, personality, and looks; performance or competence were not criteria because they were not known.

So it made sense on the surface 10 years ago to shift to a competency-based teacher-education program. Teachers could be trained in actual competencies in teaching rather than just filling their heads with knowledge about teaching. The theory of education could be translated into practice in the form of stated competencies. Some of these competencies would be knowledge and some would be performances and attitudes. But there were several questions raised by the CBTE movement that teacher educators never had to answer before. These questions are being asked and answered by the behavioristic psychologists who are the proponents of the movement. Their answers shock the humanists and traditionalists because of their rigidity.

Therefore, needless to say, the CBTE movement is controversial. The questions raised by CBTE are as follows:

- What competencies do good teachers need to have?
- What are the selection criteria for teacher trainees?
- How will the competencies be evaluated?
- Will competency-based teaching dehumanize the classroom?
- How can we measure knowledge competence?
- How can we measure pupil achievement?
- How can we account for individual differences in teaching?
- How can CBTE train teachers for differing locations—urban, rural, etc.?
- What are the levels of competency (should we expect an experienced teacher to be more competent than a beginning teacher)?
- What criteria should be used to evaluate teacher-education programs?
- How do we evaluate affective competencies?

The proponents of CBTE provide appropriate positive answers to the above questions, and the antagonists provide negative answers saying it is a passing fad and it will never work. Of course, the above questions were valid questions about teacher education long before CBTE came along—they were just never asked. So one of the major benefits of the CBTE movement has been that it has forced teacher educators to answer some hard questions about their programs.

I agree with most of the negative answers about CBTE. CBTE, in its pure behavioristic format, *does:*

- dehumanize
- force behaviorism
- try to measure nonmeasurable characteristics of excellent teaching, like warmth, enthusiasm, dedication, caring, and sense of humor
- use existing nonvalid measuring instruments for pupil achievement
- emphasize the cognitive factors over affective (humanistic) factors
- not account for individual differences
- tend to "assembly-line" teachers in the same mold
- give administrators performance measures to use to evaluate teachers
- limit learning alternatives
- make teaching and learning mechanistic and boring

But CBTE does not have to be purely behavioristic. My colleagues and I have been designing and implementing *our version* of competency-based teacher education in reading-teacher education for the past 8 years.[1] Let me illustrate what I mean by *our version*. I was invited to be on the *pro* side of a panel at the 1973 annual meeting of the National Council of Teachers of English (NCTE) entitled, "Competency-based Reading-Teacher Education, Pros and Cons." Several leaders in the field of reading were on the panel and in the audience. I was chosen to speak because I had developed an undergraduate CBTE program in reading and had published a few articles about it. The *pro* arguments were first on the agenda. I presented my program along with others. The *con* panelists then presented their arguments, but they did not use my program as an example. They had prepared their talks ahead of time and vigorously attacked the pure CBTE approach. In the discussion which followed, the *con* side panelists turned to me and said, "Don't call your program a competency-based program; it's too humanistic." They were frustrated; they came ready to attack behavioristic programs, but they encountered a program which utilized the best of the competency-based approach and the best of the Rogerian approach. *It provides freedom to learn within a clear structure.*

Following is a description of the advantages of a competency-based classroom reading specialist program.

1. *Alternatives.* Individual differences are met by providing hundreds of specifically described performance modules, each with several learning or instructional alternatives such as lectures, reading packets, classroom participation, books, demonstrations, videotapes, and audio-tapes. There are alternatives at every step; the door is always open to a new or different topic or modus operandi.

2. *Credit.* Each of the performance modules is assigned modular credit (15 modules equal one credit; a three-credit course equals 45 modules). Students choose an average of 19 performance modules to complete 45 modules of credit.

3. *Economic feasibility.* Once implemented, such a series of courses requires professor contact only in the counseling, evaluation, and lecturer roles. The courses are primarily student-directed.

4. *Multiple entry and exit points.* These courses are not bound to time. Students are done when they pass the performance modules. They are not required to attend class three times a week and take a final exam.

5. *The medium is the message.* The way we treat the undergraduates in the program, with alternatives and performance objectives, is the way we would have them treat children in an elementary school read-

ing program, giving children as much responsibility as possible for their own learning.

6. *Innovative content.* The courses include experiences in affective techniques, combating institutional racism, alternatives to standardized tests, and other components not found in traditional reading-teacher training programs.

An example of one of the learning modules for the competency statement, "The reading specialist estimates the child's actual level of reading performance," is as follows:

Module: IV, 3C, 1

Title: Informal inventories—pros and cons

Rationale: Reading specialists should have a rationale for accepting or rejecting the results of informal inventories. This module gives you the opportunity to compare and contrast inventories.

Objective: Given several different forms of informal reading inventories and given research literature concerning them, develop a one-page paper explaining the arguments for and against their use and your personal opinion pro or con.

Learning Alternatives:

1. Austin, Mary, and Huebner, Mildred, "Evaluating Progress in Reading Through Informal Procedures," in *Reading Instruction: Dimensions and Issues,* edited by William Durr, Houghton, Mifflin Co., Boston, 1967, pp. 317–327.

2. Kender, Joseph P., "Informal Reading Inventories," in Schneyer, W., "Research," *The Reading Teacher,* November 1970, pp. 165–166.

3. Harris, Albert J., "Evaluating Performance in Reading," in *How to Increase Reading Ability,* David McKay Co., Inc., New York, 1962, pp. 152–166.

4. Bond, Guy L., and Tinker, Miles A., "Informal Procedures," in *Reading Difficulties,* Appleton-Century-Crofts, New York, 1967, pp. 198–203.

5. View the videotaped lecture on informal inventories.

6. Make up your own.

Indicator: One-page paper

Evaluation: 1. The paper should indicate that the student has read at least three of the referenced works.

2. The paper should indicate that the student understands at least three arguments both for and against the use of informal inventories.

*   *   *

The entire list of 117 classroom reading-specialist competencies is available from Classroom Reading Specialist Program (grant number OEG-0-74-898), the Right to Read Office, U.S. Office of Education, Washington, D.C. 20202. My experiences with this program lead me to believe that as a format for both teachers in training and teachers in the field it offers the best chance for improving teacher training in reading. The program gives teachers a chance to diagnose their own strengths and weaknesses and to fill in the gaps.

Values education. Values education is certainly not a newcomer to the schools. One look at the old McGuffey readers would verify that. For years, though, since the days of McGuffey and since the emergence of our widely disparate population, the enforcement of the separate but equal laws, and the school prayer decision, values education has been removed from school curricula. Leave that to the family and the church, everyone agreed.

Everyone agreed until just recently, that is. Up until recently most schools knew of only one way to teach values—direct indoctrination. And the question that kept values out of the schools was: Whose values shall we teach?

Taking a look at some of the recent statistics from various sources has caused many of us to rethink the issue of teaching values. Consider these*:

a. Michigan State Police Statistics
    • In every 100 arrests for burglary in 1974, juveniles (16 and under) accounted for 45 of them.
    • Juveniles, representing only 15 percent of the population, are responsible for 41 percent of larceny arrests and 57 percent of auto-theft arrest.

b. *Ladies Home Journal* Survey
    • Among the "top 50" heroes of 5th to 12th graders were porno star Linda Lovelace and mass murderer Charles Manson.

c. Senate Sub-Committee on Juvenile Delinquency, 1974 (18 months study of 757 school districts)
    • Bill for vandalism in schools is 500 million dollars, as much as we spend on textbooks.
    • Between 1970 and 1973, the rise *in schools* were: assaults on teachers, up 75 percent; robberies, up 36 percent; and rapes, up 40 percent.

---

*Items a through f were compiled by Dr. Don Oppewal, Professor of Education, Calvin College, Grand Rapids, Mich.

d. Gallup poll of 1975 on "Public Attitudes Toward Schools"
    - Among the top 10 problems, as seen by the public: No. 1, lack of discipline; No. 6, use of drugs; and No. 8, crime/vandalism/stealing in schools.

e. Michigan State Lottery
    - A total of 450 million dollars was spent in 1975 by the public on this form of gambling.

f. Statistics from National Gun Control Center, 1976
    - There are 40,000,000 handguns in circulation in the United States.
    - Every 13 seconds a handgun is sold in the United States.
    - The United States is number one in handgun murders and accidents.
    - Sixty-nine people are shot to death every day; 25,000 every year.
    - Nearly three out of four murders are committed by friends and acquaintances.
    - Every year 10,000 people commit suicide with guns.
    - There are more gun deaths in the United States than in all other free nations combined.
    - There are 3,000 accidental firearms deaths every year.
    - Well over half of all murders are committed with handguns.
    - For every burglar who is stopped, six family members die in gun accidents.

g. Literacy
    - There are more than 18 million illiterates in the United States (USOE National Assessment of Educational Progress, 1974).
    - Twenty million adults could not read "help-wanted" ads adequately (University of Texas Adult Literacy Study, 1973).
    - An estimated 26 to 28 million adults are not able to address an envelope to insure the letter will not encounter difficulties in the postal system (University of Texas Adult Literacy Study, 1973).
    - An estimated 86 million adults were not able to calculate the gasoline consumption rate of a car (University of Texas Adult Literacy Study, 1973).

h. Television
    - Almost all Saturday morning TV ads are for sweet snack foods, likely to cause caries (American Dental Association Newsletter, September 1974).

- The average American child sees more than 250,000 TV ads by age 18 (*Learning Magazine,* December 1973).
- Ten year olds watch TV an average of 5 hours a day (National Institute for Mental Health, 1974).
- There are more TV sets in the United States than flush toilets (National Institute for Mental Health, 1974).
- A typical network ad costs $100,000; some 1-minute ads up to $250,000 (*Learning Magazine,* December 1973).

Shocking, but true, this list could contain items on poverty, hunger, violent crime, racism, and other social ills that would make one more depressed than shocked. The social problems in our country have caused educators to study the problem of teaching values rather intensively over the past few years. According to Hodgkinson,[2] there are at least six methodologies of teaching values:

1. *Direct Instruction*
   Emphasis was placed on the fact that for success this method implies and necessitates some form of social consensus and individual commitment. It is the classical mode of doctrinaire values education, and it is quite effective when prerequisite contextual conditions are present.

2. *Clarification and Analysis*
   This is the method currently popular in the literature on values education, and it tends to address, in our terms, not moral but values education.

3. *Modeling*
   The inevitability and unconscious nature of this mode were emphasized, together with the possibility of negative outcomes. The teacher is in fact a model and a values educator, and this cuts to the heart of the immaculate intermediary fallacy.

4. *Moral Reasoning*
   This method is essentially that used in the experimental course. It is the mode of dialectic and persuasion. Kohlberg's work in this methodology is classic.

5. *Dissatisfaction Induction*
   This is the method espoused and elaborated by Milton Rokeach. He argues that if a student can be shown discrepancies between his self-concept and his declared values, his values will change, directly and permanently, so as to eliminate the discrepancy.

6. *Concurrent Teaching*

This means teaching for values as well as for concepts and facts in the ordinary course of daily classroom work. It is argued that every subject can be presented in some way so that it will relate to affect and ego, and thus become a component of values education. Good teachers have been aware of this from time immemorial.

A case could be made for adopting any one of the six methodologies. I vote for number two: values clarification. Combined with the teaching of reading, I believe the values clarification approach could take us back to the McGuffey days of teaching values through reading that would be acceptable to everyone from religious zealot, to atheist, to whomever. The values clarification approach offers several pluses. They are as follows.

1. Values are not indoctrinated or taught through values clarification activities; they are clarified. Students determine what they believe; they are not told what to believe.

2. Clarifying values in a group situation tends to unify the group and make it very easy for students to talk, share, and relax.

3. It promotes a nonthreatening positive environment, since there are no right answers, no judgments, and the content is oneself.

4. Using the values-clarification approach to teaching reading comprehension promotes the highest levels of comprehension, those of application and relating the information to one's own life situation and experiences.

For the uninitiated, a simple values clarification game is "Twenty Things You Love to Do," number one in Simon's book, *Values Clarification: A Handbook of Practical Strategies for Teachers and Students.* Write down a list of things you love to do. Then code the list—a dollar sign for things that cost money, an A for things you do alone, a P for things you do with other people, and so on. Rank order the top five items on your list. Now write down next to each item how long ago you actually did the activity. This allows you to compare your attitude (value) with your behavior.

There are several other strategies. Some are moral dilemmas where you have to choose survivors or rank order wicked people, forced choice games, voting games, choose a place on a continuum between two poles, etc. Several books on the list at the end of this chapter describe such games. They are fun, exciting, relate to each individual's life, and provide endless opportunities for teaching reading comprehension.

The Larger Issue

The most promising alternatives are, as mentioned above, in teacher education. They are possible and "do-able."

There are some other ways which would produce dramatic change in reading education. They may not seem to be appropriate, but they are entirely possible in the future.

Taxpayer revolt. Parents and other taxpayers who have no children in schools (the group that is growing in number each year) will refuse to support rising school costs and teacher salaries. Laws will be passed that continue local tax support of schools, but equalize spending across urban, rural, and suburban areas. Laws will tie the funding of salaries to achievement of students and competence of teachers much the same as the "bottom-line" philosophy in business.

Federal licensure act. The federal government will license teachers based on a national board examination and standard performance criteria.

Tenure abolished. The tenure laws will be abolished and teacher performance will be judged by locally set criteria. Teachers will be evaluated by groups of parents, children, and other teachers. Teachers who do not meet the criteria will be replaced by new graduates of the Network of Federal Teacher Education Centers.

Federal teacher-education centers. All teacher education will be postgraduate work. A person with a college degree will be able to apply to one of these institutions for licensure as a teacher. Graduation from the center will require 2 years of course work and a 1-year internship. The centers will be staffed by an equal number of outstanding former teachers and outstanding former college of education professors. Similar centers will be set up in the public schools to carry on federally supported educational research.

Once these new laws and centers are established and the new cabinet-level, national department of education reviews the failures and successes, more action will be taken to insure that every child has the right to learn to read. Some believe that only then will we begin to end the literacy crisis in America.

Reading teachers, classroom teachers, and reading professors across the country are experimenting, changing, and growing in various ways. As more and more continue to understand the complexities of The Great American Reading Machine, illiteracy will begin to be eradicated. We need to continue to take bold risks, persevere, make some mistakes, and grow in our knowledge of what works. For now, reading instruction is as good as the teacher your child has today. You be the judge.

References

1. Yarington, David J., Boffey, Barnes, Evans, Martha, Earle, Richard, and Schreck, William, *Classroom Reading Specialist Program*, 4, volumes, USOE Year-end Report, Grant No. OEG-0-74-8981, July 1975, 742 pp. The components were authored by the following persons:

Volume I

Guide for the Implementor

I	Reading/Language Arts, K–12	D. Barnes Boffey and David J. Yarington

Volume II

II	Readiness and Beginning Reading	Martha Evans
III	Comprehension	Richard Earle
IV	Diagnosis	David J. Yarington
V	Learning/Study Styles	David J. Yarington
VI	The Future: Trial/Error Teaching/Learning	David J. Yarington

Volume III

VII	Administration and Supervision	Richard Earle
VIII	Remediation and Clinical Practicum	David J. Yarington
IX	The Affective Domain	D. Barnes Boffey

Volume IV

X	Process—Theory and Practice	Martha Evans
XI	Research and Measurement	Martha Evans
XII	Survival Skills	D. Barnes Boffey
XIII	Presentation Skills	David J. Yarington
XIV	Sexism and Racism	William R. Schreck, Jr.

2. Hodgkinson, Christopher, "Values Education at One Remove," *Phi Delta Kappan*, vol. 58, November 1976, pp. 270–271.

Readings in Humanistic and Values Education

1. Casteel, J. Doyle, and Stahl, Robert J., *Value Clarification in the Classroom: A Primer*, Goodyear Publishing Company, Inc., Pacific Palisades, Calif., 1975.

2. Chase, Larry, *The Other Side of the Report Card: A How-to-Do-It Program for Affective Education,* Goodyear Publishing Company, Inc., Pacific Palisades, Calif., 1975.

3. Council on Interracial Books for Children, *Human (and Anti-Human) Values in Children's Books,* CIBC Racism and Sexism Resource Center for Educators, New York, 1976.

4. Curwin, Rick, et al., *Search for Values, Dimensions of Personality,* a book of ditto masters for values clarification games and an instructor's book. Pflaum/Standard, Dayton, Ohio, 1972.

5. Foster, Herbert L., *Ribbin', Jivin', and Playin' the Dozens: The Unrecognized Dilemma of Inner City Schools,* Ballinger Publishing Co., Cambridge, Mass., 1974.

6. Frazier, Nancy, and Sadker, Myra, *Sexism in School and Society,* Harper & Row, New York, 1973.

7. Harmin, Merrill, Kirschenbaum, Howard, and Simon, Sidney B., *Clarifying Values Through Subject Matter: Applications for the Classroom,* Winston Press, Inc., Minneapolis, Minn. 1973.

8. Hawley, Robert C., and Hawley, Isabel L., *A Handbook of Personal Growth Activities for Classroom Use,* Education Research Associates, Amherst, Mass., 1972.

9. Heath, Douglas, *Humanizing Schools: New Directions, New Decisions,* Hayden Book Company, Inc., Rochelle Park, N.J., 1971.

10. Howe, Leland W., and Howe, Mary Martha, *Personalizing Education: Values Clarification and Beyond,* Hart Publishing Company, Inc., New York, 1975.

11. Insel, Paul M., *What Do You Expect? An Inquiry into Self-Fulfilling Prophecies,* Cummings Publishing Company, Inc., Menlo Park, Calif., 1975.

12. Johnson, David W., *Reaching Out,* Prentice-Hall, Inc., Englewood Cliffs, N.J., 1972.

13. Kirschenbaum, Howard, and Simon, Sidney B., *Readings in Values Clarification,* Winston Press, Inc., Minneapolis, Minn., 1973.

14. Lyon, Harold C. Jr., *Learning to Feel—Feeling to Learn: Humanistic Education for the Whole Man,* Charles E. Merrill Publishing Co., Columbus, Ohio, 1971.

15. Macrorie, Ken, *A Vulnerable Teacher,* Hayden Book Company, Inc., Rochelle Park, N.J., 1974.

16. Macrorie, Ken, *Uptaught,* Hayden Book Company, Inc., Rochelle Park, N.J., 1970.

17. Miller, John P., *Humanizing the Classroom: Models of Teaching in Affective Education,* Praeger Publishing, Inc., New York, 1976.

18. Raths, Louis E., Harmin, Merrill, and Simon, Sidney B., *Values and Teaching: Working with Values in the Classroom,* Charles E. Merrill Publishing Co., Columbus, Ohio, 1971.

19. Read, Donald A., and Simon, Sidney B., *Humanistic Education Sourcebook*, Prentice-Hall, Inc., Englewood Cliffs, N.J., 1975.
20. Rogers, Carl R., *Freedom to Learn*, Charles E. Merrill Publishing Co., Columbus Ohio, 1969.
21. Ruben, Brent D., and Budd, Richard W., *Human Communication Handbook: Simulations and Games*, vols. 1 and 2, Hayden Book Company, Inc., Rochelle Park, N.J., 1975.
22. Rutstein, Nat, *Go Watch TV! What and How Much Should Children Really Watch?*, Sheed & Ward, Inc., New York, 1974.
23. Satir, Virginia, *Peoplemaking*, Science and Behavior Books, Inc., Palo Alto, Calif., 1972.
24. Schrank, Jeffrey, *Teaching Human Beings: 101 Subversive Activities for the Classroom*, Beacon Press, Boston, 1972.
25. Seaberg, Dorothy I., *The Four Faces of Teaching: The Role of the Teacher in Humanizing Education*, Goodyear Publishing Company, Pacific Palisades, Calif., 1974.
26. Simon, Sidney B., *I Am Loveable and Capable: A Modern Allegory on the Classical Put-Down*, Argus Communications, Niles, Ill., 1974.
27. Simon, Sidney B., *Meeting Yourself Halfway: 31 Value Clarification Strategies for Daily Living*, Argus Communications, Niles, Ill., 1974.
28. Simon, Sidney B., Howe, Leland W., and Kirschenbaum, Howard, *Values Clarification: A Handbook of Practical Strategies for Teachers and Students*, Hart Publishing Company, Inc., New York, 1972.
29. Simon, Sidney B., Hawley, Robert C., and Britton, David D., *Composition for Personal Growth: Values Clarification Through Writing*. Hart Publishing Company, Inc., New York, 1973.

TRAITS OF
COMPETENT TEACHERS*

Broad Range of Experience

A teacher who has had a broad range of experience could be described by some of the following:

He is able to communicate and interpret different methods of organizing data. He sees varied answers to and perceptions of a problem and responds in kind rather than considering divergent answers or perceptions as being wrong. Stuff of all sorts is around: paintings, mobiles, art work, musical instruments, exhibits, and books on different subjects. During lessons he shares his background. He brings in many outside-of-the-classroom people. He takes children on more-than-routine trips, beyond the firehouse and post office. His planning is flexible and he has a different curriculum each semester.

Sensitivity

A teacher who is sensitive could be described by some of the following:

She shows gentle strength. She holds control to allow individual attention to special needs and positions of children. She listens-sees-feels, i.e., she fully senses the reality of the moment and reacts, at the moment. She responds with direct eye contact and motion, not sitting or standing in one spot. She is aware of her ability to make and repair mistakes. She is constantly aware of being fair. She is empathetic. She knows and reacts to the needs of each child as a person with rights, feelings, thoughts, and needs. She respects and listens to each child as an individual, not as a "type." She gives an honest, personal response to the questions and actions of each child.

*See Chap. 5, p. 63.

Lack of Bias

A teacher who is unbiased could be described by some of the following:

He allows diverse ideas and encourages controversy. Students are encouraged to talk and their ideas are acknowledged. He listens without interrupting and without preconceptions about answers given by such a "type." He does not allow favoritism to interfere with fairness. He can be seen responding with physical affection to all children at different times and when it is appropriate. He asks questions to which he has no right answers. He accepts answers on a wide spectrum without being overly rewarding or punishing. He helps all children move on at an optimum rate (doesn't give easy holding-back work to kids he might assume are slow). He notices and supports, by word or by nonverbal messages, positive growth in all children. He is aware of his own values, states opposing viewpoints to the satisfaction of adherents, and is encouraging even when disagreeing.

Flexibility

A teacher who is flexible could be described by some of the following:

She listens-sees-feels, i.e., she fully senses the reality of the moment. She has an awareness of her environment (society, communal, class) at the moment in time, and she adjusts her own behavior to function most effectively within the environment to her own purposes. She can attack a given situation in many different ways. She is a good brainstormer, creative problem solver, and has a wide vocabulary that allows a range of expression. There are many instances where she starts one thought and switches to another midstream. She prefers a partly open schedule to merely courses and "slave learnings." She is able to: write a list of 20 interests in 4 minutes, get a pass–fail card OK'd in 30 minutes. She functions well in many different roles required by school. Her open-mindedness to new ideas is exemplified by her willingness to try new teaching techniques and procedures. She can easily change her lesson plans when circumstances indicate other plans are in order. She can deal with various speech patterns. She does not react to particular student behaviors with set patterned responses. She matches instruction to learner aptitudes, rather then forcing one mode of instruction for all students. She uses many materials to accomplish the same task. She encourages divergent behavior and thinking and asks many open-ended questions. She can pose 10 to 15 questions about any action, material, etc., in about 5 minutes. She uses discipline without being a disciplinarian. Her recess activities vary every day.

Concern for Children's Growth

A teacher who is concerned for children's growth could be described by some of the following:

His general orientation is toward the release of each child's potential and not toward the solution or exploration of his own problems. He recognizes and is involved with kids' emotions. He and the children openly share feelings: fear, excitement, joy, depression, sorrow, concern, etc. They hold and practice mutual respect for each other's ideas, concerns, feelings, efforts, and needs. In the classroom a feeling of trust and caring pervades. Much of the interchange is originated from the student to other students, and from the student to the teacher. It looks like a community of involvement as children are seen helping, teaching, planning, and loving each other. There are full relationships. Ideas initiated by children are heard and encouraged by the teacher and other students. He is able to provide praise and success for the student as an individual, which is not totally determined by the confines of the teacher's own course objectives. He attempts to relate to, befriend, and love other persons. His understanding of the learning process and human growth and development allows him to explore different learning experiences. He has a perspective on the importance of his academic discipline and why it is important to the individual student.

Sense of Humor

A teacher who has a sense of humor could be described by some of the following:

She shows a sense of proportion regarding her own importance. She sees the closeness of tragedy and comedy and does not confuse sincerity and humor. She smiles easily and naturally. She can see absurdity in much human activity without hostility or condescension toward the humans involved. People have fun being around her and she has fun being with people. She can laugh at herself and her weaknesses. She is a good ad libber, can banter, and can also be sincere. It is common to hear laughter in her classroom by both her and her students, but she does not provoke laughter at the expense of someone else. A student is not made the butt of jokes or comments. She laughs at situations, not people. Laughing with, rather than at, is encouraged.

Students are not chewed out for laughing in class. Potentially embarrassing situations are turned into humorous ones. She truly enjoys being with children.

Self-Awareness

A teacher who is self-aware could be described by some of the following:

He is conscious of his own vitality, sexiness, life urges, and energies. He is conscious of and able to articulate his needs, depressions, anxieties, or weak areas. He is conscious of, but not obsessed with, his interaction with others. He understands the attributes of any particular situation and chooses his actions appropriately according to his own desires and needs. He has the ability to understand his own reactions to situations and people as related to his own self-concept. He displays confidence in his walk, his smiles, his snarls, his frowns, his warmth, and his understanding. He expresses verbal confidence in himself. He has the ability to repair mistakes.

Strong Self-Concept

A teacher who has a strong self-concept could be described by some of the following:

She shows her independence in thoughts, feelings, and actions. She has confidence in her own beliefs and actions. She doesn't turn back questions; she takes a position. In conversations, she says more than, "What do you think?" She doesn't feel everything has to be justified, explained, or apologized for, and she articulates her own strengths and weaknesses without apology. She is serene and enjoys solitude. She does not make self-deprecatory statements, and if she is nervous, she admits it. She is optimistic and cheerfully accepts personal setbacks. She can recognize and deal with her limitations and still like herself. In the classroom, she accepts failure and learns from mistakes. She is not afraid to say, "I don't know the answer." She is eager to share and explore her own ideas with others. She is aware of the person with whom she is speaking, not of others and her impression on them. Others do not easily frighten her, or she is not swayed by them just because she wants to be accepted. She is cheerful when she gets up in the morning and walks and stands with confidence and looks at ease with herself. She often sings and whistles. She'll give an opinion different from the four people who spoke first and agreed, if she differs. She is known by name rather than as "the teacher."

Enthusiasm

A teacher who is enthusiastic could be described by some of the following:

He is spirited, optimistic, bouncy, happy, and lively. He moves around the room and works hard without getting tired quickly. He has a high energy level. Children and adults enjoy being with him and want to share their thoughts, ideas, and experiences with him. He shares the fact that he is interested and learns in the classroom along with the children and is eager to motivate children to want to learn and enjoy learning. He can see how others can be enthusiastic about things in which he is unenthusiastic. His relationships go beyond the limits of space and time of the classroom. He really enjoys children, teaching, self, classroom, learning, and can and does show it. He has the ability to dream up interesting things to do, but is not disappointed when others don't share interests, as the enthusiasm is genuine. He tries a new idea a second time even if it was a bust the first time. He is alert and aware and really with the situation, the child, the adult. He follows through on something even if it is not in the curriculum. He is alert to ways of expressing his interests and ideas and talks readily about his interests and ideas. He speaks in different voice ranges. He takes risks and is willing to go out on a limb.

Desire to Teach

A teacher who has a strong desire to teach could be described by some of the following:

She enjoys using her head and heart and body to help others. She enjoys getting resources and people together. She understands the structure of knowledge and how people learn. She wants to continue to learn and share learning and is interested in learning as in teaching. Her long range plans include continued education in the field; she wants to improve as a professional. She wishes to teach at various grade levels. She has gone out of her way to have meaningful contact with children. She has worked in camps, playgrounds, or Head Start or as a tutor, etc. She really loves and enjoys being with children and feels relationships and friendships made with them are no less important than those made with her peers. She understands the pitfalls of the profession: politics, frustrations, ego trips, administration, hours, parents, etc. She doesn't complain about recordkeeping. She understands that teaching isn't all like a storybook, with kids bringing you apples and flowers. After strongly considering other vocations, she can recognize and analyze her own reasons for wanting to teach. She is motivated by other than vacations, family, job security, easy major, etc. She is anticipating action when observing cooperative teachers. She begins her practice teaching within 2 days. She is willing to plan her own lessons when practice teaching and rarely uses the same lesson plan more than once. She is willing to spend her free time improving the classroom environment. She is seldom absent from school and isn't always the first one out of the building at the close of school. She is able to work with principals whose philosophy of education differs from hers. She is motivated by a generous belief in education and a respect for students based on experiences with children.

Warmth

A teacher who is warm could be described by some of the following:

He is open and nondefensive. He accepts other people and speaks to them, rather than at or to the side of them. He is interested and pays attention to the children. He has a kindly, good-natured way of talking to people during class. He laughs, he smiles, he makes children feel that they are welcome in his classroom. He chats socially with the children. There is a feeling of friendliness between him and the students. He is considerate of his pupils and would put aside his own work if asked for advice about personal problems.

Honesty

A teacher who is honest could be described by some of the following:

She can express feelings and emotions easily. She can say, "I don't know," "I want," "I need." She maintains confidentiality. She praises student honesty. She admits mistakes, declares her feelings when they are operating to avoid hidden agendas, and states her own positions on issues. You know where she stands. She deals with the reality of any situation or question that comes up by searching out all sides, cognitive or otherwise. She talks openly and listens openly. She doesn't brush things aside and data is not used in pieces. She lets the kids in on games she plays and follows up on promises she makes. She is straightforward and trusts people. She questions often: authorities, her own fundamental assumptions, and the people she loves. She has the same "face" for all groups. She takes responsibility for her own behavior and positions. She has a consistent set of values. She is un-afraid of confrontation or hassling with people. There is a focus on ideas, rather than ego investment.

INDEX

INDEX

179